C000112992

NEW ZEALAND

Graeme Lay

NEW HOLLAND

New Holland Publishers (UK) Ltd
London • Auckland • Cape Town • Sydney
10 9 8 7 6 5 4 3 2 1

First edition   2007

www.newhollandpublishers.com

Garfield House, 86 Edgware Road
London W2 2EA, United Kingdom

218 Lake Road
Northcote, Auckland, New Zealand

80 McKenzie Street
Cape Town 8001, South Africa

14 Aquatic Drive
Frenchs Forest, NSW 2086, Australia

Distributed in the USA by
The Globe Pequot Press, Connecticut

ISBN 978 1 84537 445 7

Publishing Manager: Thea Grobbelaar
DTP Cartographic Manager: Genené Hart
Editor: Nicky Steenkamp
Designers: Genené Hart, Nicole Bannister
Cartographer: Genené Hart
Cartographic Assistant: Tanja Spinola
Picture Research: Shavonne Govender
New Zealand Consultants: Anna Craig,
Dee Murch
Proofreader: Thea Grobbelaar

Reproduction by Resolution, Cape Town
Printed and bound by Times Offset (M)
Sdn. Bhd., Malaysia.

Photographic Credits:
Gerald Cubitt: pages 15, 19 (top),
40, 44, 58 (right), 62 (bottom), 72,
78, 80 (right);
Peter Adams/jonarnoldimages.com:
page 60 (top);
Jon Arnold/jonarnoldimages.com:
pages 17, 18, 19 (bottom), 28, 30, 32,
42, 48 (top and bottom), 60 (bottom),
64 (top), 74, 76;
Joe Malone/jonarnoldimages.com:
title page;
Doug Pearson/jonarnoldimages.com:
imprint page, pages 12, 13, 14, 16,
21, 22 (bottom), 24, 25, 26, 27, 38
(top and botom), 50 (top), 56 (top),
58 (left), 66 (top and bottom), 68;
Bob McCree: pages 10, 20, 33, 36
(bottom), 50 (bottom), 54 (left and
right), 56 (bottom), 62 (top), 64
(bottom), 70;
Neil Setchfield: pages 8, 22 (top),
46, 52;
Jeroen Snijders: pages 36 (top),
80 (left);
Rob Suisted: cover.

Cover: *Aoraki/Mount Cook, at 3754m,
is New Zealand's highest mountain.*
Title page: *Traditional Maori carved wall
panel in Rotorua.*
Below: *Mount Taranaki, at 2518m, dominates
the landscape of Taranaki province.*

CONTENTS

TOURIST AREAS

INDEX

For ease of use, the Index has been divided into two sections:

• the first focuses on the Tourist Area Maps and related text and photographs.

• the second deals with the Main Map Section only, facilitating the easy location of cities, towns and villages.

MAIN MAP SECTION

National Route Planner

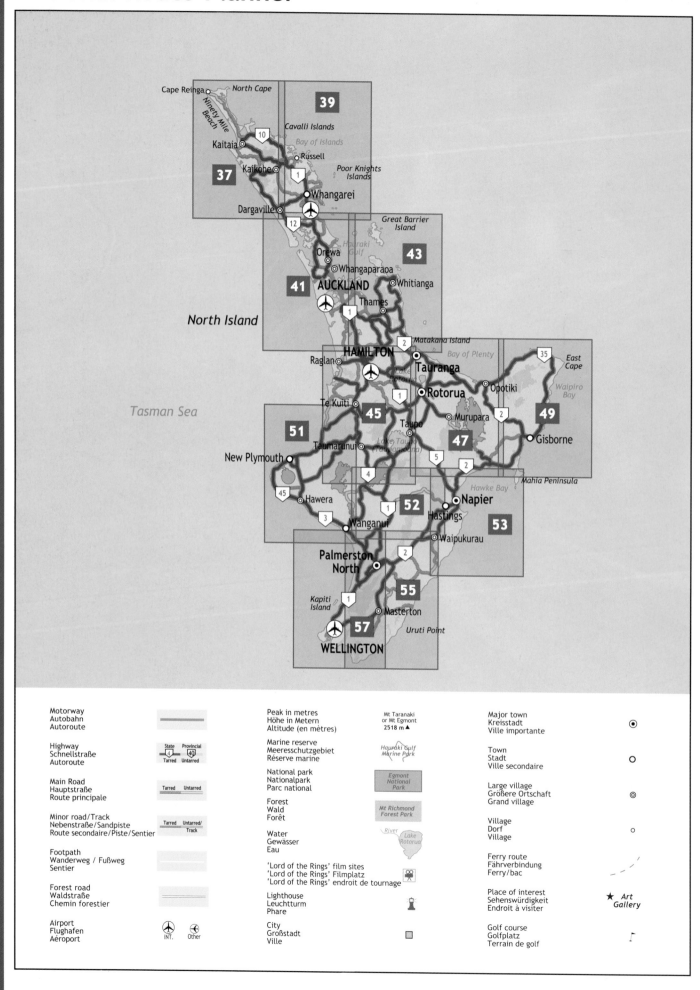

Legend

Motorway
Autobahn
Autoroute

Highway
Schnellstraße
Autoroute
State 4 Provincial 40
Tarred   Untarred

Main Road
Hauptstraße
Route principale
Tarred   Untarred

Minor road/Track
Nebenstraße/Sandpiste
Route secondaire/Piste/Sentier
Tarred   Untarred/Track

Footpath
Wanderweg / Fußweg
Sentier

Forest road
Waldstraße
Chemin forestier

Airport
Flughafen
Aéroport
INT.   Other

Peak in metres
Höhe in Metern
Altitude (en mètres)
Mt Taranaki or Mt Egmont
2518 m ▲

Marine reserve
Meeresschutzgebiet
Réserve marine
Hauraki Gulf Marine Park

National park
Nationalpark
Parc national
Egmont National Park

Forest
Wald
Forêt
Mt Richmond Forest Park

Water
Gewässer
Eau
River   Lake Rotorua

'Lord of the Rings' film sites
'Lord of the Rings' Filmplatz
'Lord of the Rings' endroit de tournage

Lighthouse
Leuchtturm
Phare

City
Großstadt
Ville

Major town
Kreisstadt
Ville importante
⊙

Town
Stadt
Ville secondaire
○

Large village
Größere Ortschaft
Grand village
◉

Village
Dorf
Village
○

Ferry route
Fährverbindung
Ferry/bac

Place of interest
Sehenswürdigkeit
Endroit à visiter
★ Art Gallery

Golf course
Golfplatz
Terrain de golf

National Route Planner

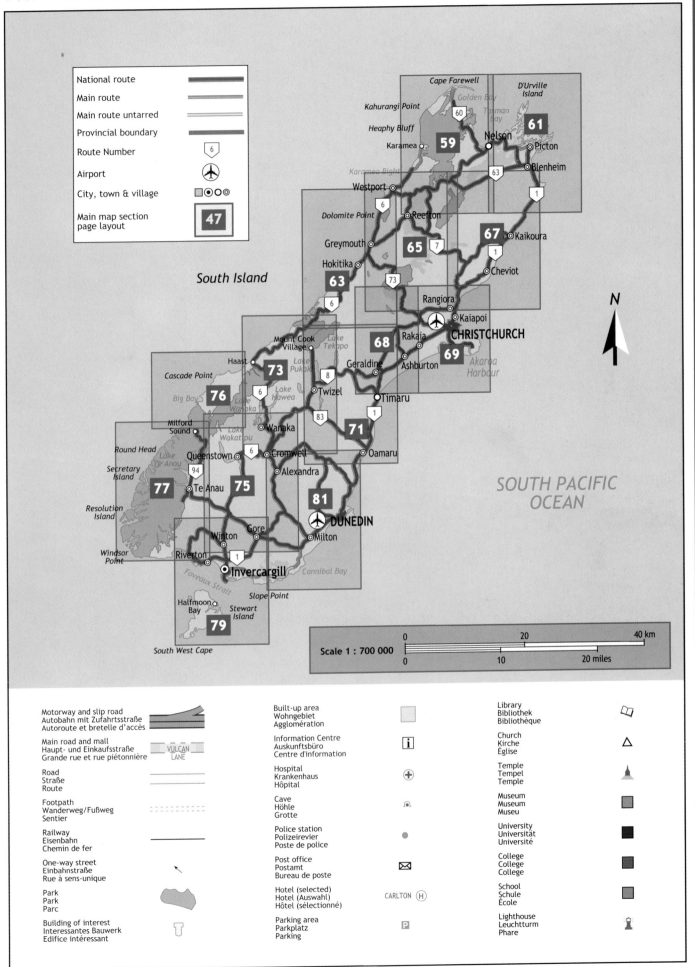

Legend (top)

National route	
Main route	
Main route untarred	
Provincial boundary	
Route Number	6
Airport	✈
City, town & village	▢ ◉ ○ ◎
Main map section page layout	47

South Island

Cape Farewell
D'Urville Island
Kahurangi Point
Golden Bay
Tasman Bay
Heaphy Bluff
60
Nelson
61
Karamea
59
Picton
Karamea Bight
63
Blenheim
Westport
6
Reefton
Dolomite Point
7
1
Greymouth
65
67 Kaikoura
Hokitika
73
1
Cheviot
63
Rangiora
6
Kaiapoi
Mount Cook Village
Lake Tekapo
68 Rakaia CHRISTCHURCH
Haast
73
Lake Pukaki
Geraldine
69
Cascade Point
8
Ashburton
Akaroa Harbour
Big Bay
6
Twizel
Lake Hawea
Timaru
76
83
1
Milford Sound
Lake Wanaka
71
Round Head
Wanaka
Oamaru
Secretary Island
Lake Wakatipu
Queenstown
6
Cromwell
SOUTH PACIFIC OCEAN
94
Alexandra
77
75
Resolution Island
Te Anau
81
Windsor Point
Winton
Gore
DUNEDIN
Riverton
Milton
1
Foveaux Strait
Invercargill
Cannibal Bay
Slope Point
Halfmoon Bay
Stewart Island
79
South West Cape

N

Scale 1 : 700 000

0   20   40 km
0   10   20 miles

Legend (bottom)

Motorway and slip road / Autobahn mit Zufahrtsstraße / Autoroute et bretelle d'accès		Built-up area / Wohngebiet / Agglomération		Library / Bibliothek / Bibliothèque
Main road and mall / Haupt- und Einkaufsstraße / Grande rue et rue piétonnière (VULCAN LANE)		Information Centre / Auskunftsbüro / Centre d'information	i	Church / Kirche / Église
Road / Straße / Route		Hospital / Krankenhaus / Hôpital	⊕	Temple / Tempel / Temple
Footpath / Wanderweg/Fußweg / Sentier		Cave / Höhle / Grotte		Museum / Museum / Museu
Railway / Eisenbahn / Chemin de fer		Police station / Polizeirevier / Poste de police	●	University / Universität / Université
One-way street / Einbahnstraße / Rue à sens-unique		Post office / Postamt / Bureau de poste	✉	College / College / College
Park / Park / Parc		Hotel (selected) / Hotel (Auswahl) / Hôtel (sélectionné)	CARLTON (H)	School / Schule / École
Building of interest / Interessantes Bauwerk / Edifice intéressant		Parking area / Parkplatz / Parking	P	Lighthouse / Leuchtturm / Phare

Tourist Area Planner

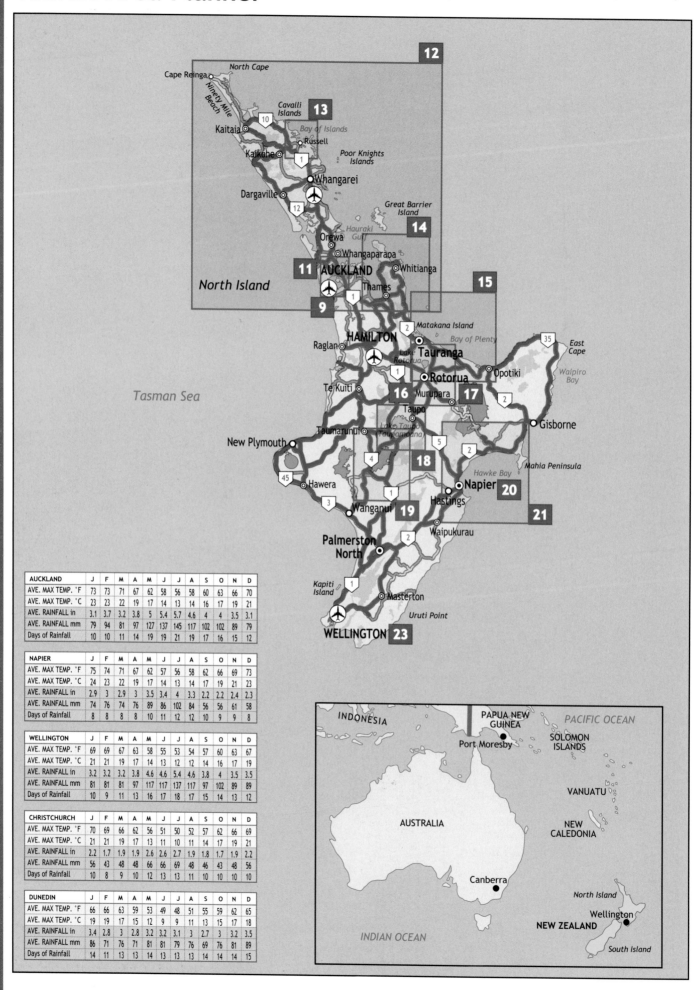

AUCKLAND	J	F	M	A	M	J	J	A	S	O	N	D
AVE. MAX TEMP. °F	73	73	71	67	62	58	56	58	60	63	66	70
AVE. MAX TEMP. °C	23	23	22	19	17	14	13	14	16	17	19	21
AVE. RAINFALL in	3.1	3.7	3.2	3.8	5	5.4	5.7	4.6	4	4	3.5	3.1
AVE. RAINFALL mm	79	94	81	97	127	137	145	117	102	102	89	79
Days of Rainfall	10	10	11	14	19	19	21	19	17	16	15	12

NAPIER	J	F	M	A	M	J	J	A	S	O	N	D
AVE. MAX TEMP. °F	75	74	71	67	62	57	56	58	62	66	69	73
AVE. MAX TEMP. °C	24	23	22	19	17	14	13	14	17	19	21	23
AVE. RAINFALL in	2.9	3	2.9	3	3.5	3.4	4	3.3	2.2	2.2	2.4	2.3
AVE. RAINFALL mm	74	76	74	76	89	86	102	84	56	56	61	58
Days of Rainfall	8	8	8	8	10	11	12	12	10	9	9	8

WELLINGTON	J	F	M	A	M	J	J	A	S	O	N	D
AVE. MAX TEMP. °F	69	69	67	63	58	55	53	54	57	60	63	67
AVE. MAX TEMP. °C	21	21	19	17	14	13	12	12	14	16	17	19
AVE. RAINFALL in	3.2	3.2	3.2	3.8	4.6	4.6	5.4	4.6	3.8	4	3.5	3.5
AVE. RAINFALL mm	81	81	81	97	117	117	137	117	97	102	89	89
Days of Rainfall	10	9	11	13	16	17	18	17	15	14	13	12

CHRISTCHURCH	J	F	M	A	M	J	J	A	S	O	N	D
AVE. MAX TEMP. °F	70	69	66	62	56	51	50	52	57	62	66	69
AVE. MAX TEMP. °C	21	21	19	17	13	11	10	11	14	17	19	21
AVE. RAINFALL in	2.2	1.7	1.9	1.9	2.6	2.6	2.7	1.9	1.8	1.7	1.9	2.2
AVE. RAINFALL mm	56	43	48	48	66	66	69	48	46	43	48	56
Days of Rainfall	10	8	9	10	12	13	13	10	10	10	10	10

DUNEDIN	J	F	M	A	M	J	J	A	S	O	N	D
AVE. MAX TEMP. °F	66	66	63	59	53	49	48	51	55	59	62	65
AVE. MAX TEMP. °C	19	19	17	15	12	9	9	11	13	15	17	18
AVE. RAINFALL in	3.4	2.8	3	2.8	3.2	3.2	3.1	3	2.7	3	3.2	3.5
AVE. RAINFALL mm	86	71	76	71	81	81	79	76	69	76	81	89
Days of Rainfall	14	11	13	13	14	13	13	14	14	14	14	15

Tourist Area Planner

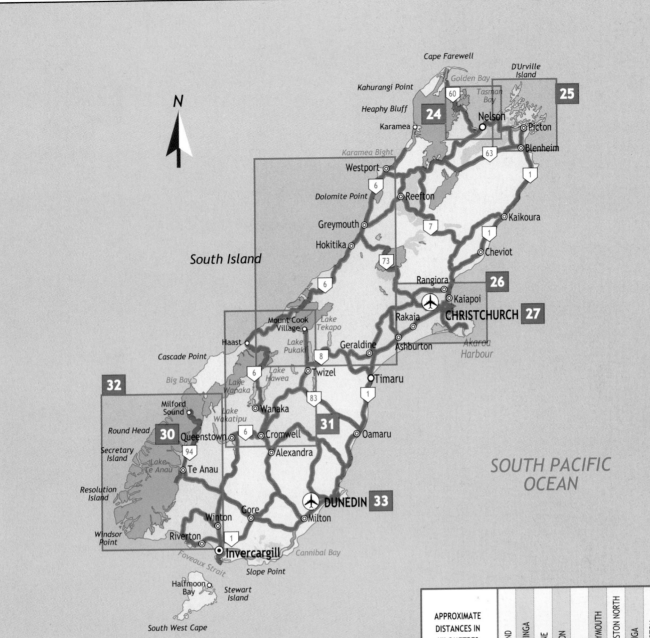

South Island

SOUTH PACIFIC OCEAN

Legend

National route	
Main route	
Main route untarred	
Provincial boundary	
Route Number	6
Airport	✈
City, town & village	▣ ◉ ○ ◎
Main map section page layout	30

APPROXIMATE DISTANCES IN KILOMETRES	AUCKLAND	CAPE REINGA	GISBORNE	HAMILTON	NAPIER	NEW PLYMOUTH	PALMERSTON NORTH	TAURANGA	WELLINGTON
AUCKLAND		440	507	127	422	366	530	208	656
CAPE REINGA	440		943	566	861	805	967	645	1100
DARGAVILLE	185	285	685	312	605	554	713	390	845
GISBORNE	507	943		394	215	600	390	300	540
HAMILTON	127	566	394		295	242	402	108	533
HICKS BAY	508	945	180	398	396	600	574	302	730
KAITAIA	325	114	827	450	748	692	853	535	982
MASTERTON	638	1077	448	511	233	343	109	530	100
NAPIER	422	861	215	295		412	178	312	320
NEW PLYMOUTH	366	805	600	242	412		234	308	355
PAIHIA	241	220	745	368	664	610	773	447	900
PALMERSTON NORTH	530	967	390	402	178	234		420	145
ROTORUA	235	672	292	109	227	315	340	86	460
TAUPO	280	720	335	153	143	296	259	165	378
TAUMARUNUI	295	726	450	162	264	183	240	230	360
TAURANGA	208	645	300	108	312	308	420		545
THAMES	115	554	413	106	360	348	470	114	586
WAIOURU	423	819	446	267	261	288	145	279	264
WANGANUI	454	893	466	328	252	160	74	439	195
WELLINGTON	656	1100	540	533	320	355	145	545	
WHANGAREI	170	270	680	295	597	540	700	381	818

Auckland Area

With a population of 1,318,700 — 32% of the country's total — Auckland is by far New Zealand's largest, and fastest-growing, city. Built across the Tamaki Isthmus, between the Waitemata and Manukau harbours, the city's suburbs extend 40km from north to south and from the Waitakere Ranges in the west to Waiheke Island in the east. A harbour bridge connects the southern and northern shores of the Waitemata Harbour. The central isthmus is studded with extinct volcanic cones, most of which are reserves, and the coast is fringed with beaches. Auckland is an increasingly cosmopolitan, multicultural city with a large immigrant population.

Right: *Devonport (foreground), Waitemata Harbour and the central business district of Auckland city.*

MAIN ATTRACTIONS

- The views from the summit of one of the city's **volcanic cones** e.g. **Mount Victoria**, **North Head**, **Mount Eden** or **Rangitoto Island**.
- The views of Auckland from the observation deck of the **Sky Tower** (328m) are spectacular.
- A **ferry trip** across the **Waitemata Harbour** to the **Victorian-era village** of **Devonport**.
- **Wine tasting** at one of the vineyards on **Waiheke Island** (*see* map p. 41).
- **The Auckland War Memorial Museum** in the Domain contains a collection of Maoritanga, Polynesian and Melanesian artefacts.
- A meal at one of the **Viaduct Basin's** many harbourside restaurants, located on the site of a formerly run-down area of the waterfront.
- A visit to **Kelly Tarlton's Antarctic Encounter and Underwater World**.
- The **22 regional parks** which surround the Auckland region.

TRAVEL TIPS

Stagecoach Auckland: timetable enquiries, MAXX (09) 366 6400 or call free: 0800 782 432, website: www.stagecoach.co.nz
The Link Bus connects the inner city suburbs of Parnell, Ponsonby and Newmarket with Queen Street.
Auckland Airport is located 19.5km southwest of the central city. An Airbus connects the city's domestic and international terminals with Downtown Auckland's main hotels. The bus leaves for the airport every twenty minutes from Quay Street, opposite the Ferry Building, during the day and every thirty

minutes during the evening. Travel time to the airport from the city is about 40 minutes.
A **free bus** which leaves every few minutes from outside the terminals connects Auckland's domestic and international terminals. There is also a walkway joining the two.
Auckland Explorer Bus. One or two days. An easy way to explore Auckland's top visitor attractions, on a double-decker bus. Get on and off the bus as you please.
Auckland Pass. A one-day pass for one person for all-day use of all Stagecoach and Link buses and North Shore-

Downtown Fullers Ferries.
All travel information can be obtained at any of the city's **i-SITE Visitor Centres** located at:
Atrium SKYCITY: Victoria Street; 137 Quay Street, Princes Wharf.
International Airport: Ground Floor Arrivals Hall.
Devonport Visitor Centre: 3 Victoria Road, Devonport, website: www.aucklandnz.com
North Shore City Information: tel: (09) 486 8600.
Emergency Services (Police, Fire, Ambulance): 111.

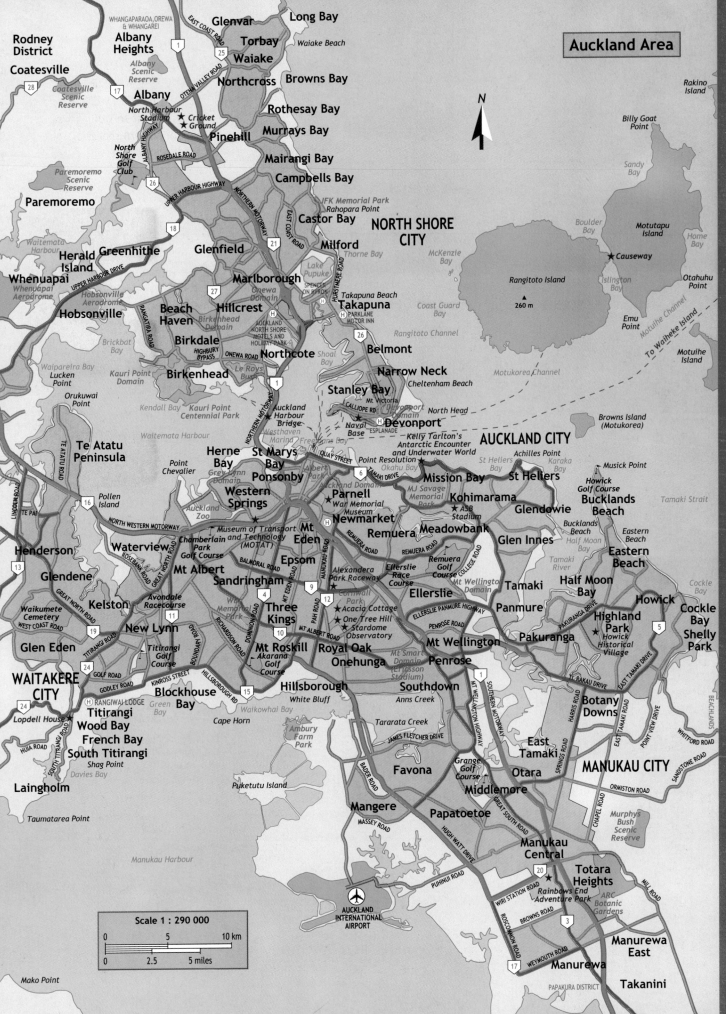

Auckland City

The city's central business district is located along the lower half of Queen Street, which occupies a valley between two ridges and which runs down to the Waitemata Harbourfront. Banks, insurance companies, movie theatres, department stores, gift shops, hotels and food halls are located in Queen Street. Most of the best quality shopping is located in other areas, notably High Street, Vulcan Lane, Karangahape Road, Newmarket, Parnell, Ponsonby and Devonport. Albert Park, above Kitchener Street, is a lovely expanse of lawns, paths and mature trees. The city Art Gallery is located in the southwest corner of Albert Park. The Viaduct Basin is a district of shops, restaurants, apartments and pleasure boat moorings, the entrance to which is from Lower Hobson Street.

ACCOMMODATION

Hyatt Regency Auckland: cnr Princes Street and Waterloo Quadrant, tel: (09) 355 1234, fax: (09) 303 2932, e-mail: auckland@hyatt.co.nz website: www.auckland.regency.hyatt.com A few minutes' walk from Queen Street and close to the Old Government House and Albert Park.

Hilton Auckland: 147 Quay Street, tel: (09) 978 2000, international free-phone: 1800 445 8667, NZ freephone: 0800 448 002, fax: (09) 978 2001, e-mail: reservations.auckland@hilton.com A boutique-style hotel located at the end of Princes Wharf.

The Spencer on Byron Hotel: 9–17 Byron Avenue, Takapuna, tel: (09) 916 6111, fax: (09) 916 6110, e-mail: reservations@spencerbyron.co.nz website: www.spencerbyron.co.nz In the heart of Takapuna, on the city's North Shore, with views over Takapuna Beach and Rangitoto Island.

Esplanade Hotel: 1 Victoria Road, Devonport, tel: (09) 445 1291, fax: (09) 445 1999, e-mail: reservations@esplanadehotel.co.nz website: www.esplanadehotel.co.nz A restored Edwardian hotel on the waterfront at Devonport.

Left: One of the many restaurants on Princes Wharf, near the Viaduct Basin. There are literally rows of restaurants in the main eating-out districts around the Viaduct Basin and similarly at Mission Bay, on the eastern waterfront.

MAIN ATTRACTIONS

- A visit to **Auckland Zoo**, where visitors will see hippos, lions and primates as well as New Zealand natives, the kiwi and tuatara.
- Strolling around the **Viaduct Basin** and lunching at one of its restaurants.
- A **picnic** lunch in **Albert Park**, followed by a visit to the **Auckland Art Gallery.**

- **Coffee** and **shopping** in Parnell, Ponsonby or Newmarket.
- **Parnell Baths**, the city's only public saltwater pool.
- Shopping at the **Victoria Park Market**, in Victoria Park West.
- A **cruise** on the **Waitemata Harbour** on a launch or an ex-America's Cup yacht.
- A trip to **Queen Street's Civic Theatre**, built in 1929, and which has been restored to glory in recent times.

Scale 1: 18 000

Auckland City

Breakwater

Northern Motorway

Point Erin Park

Westhaven Marina

St Marys Bay

Ferry to Birkenhead
Ferry to Bayswater
Ferry to Stanley Bay
Ferry to Devonport
Waitemata Harbour

Wynyard Wharf
Freemans Bay
Princes Wharf Passenger Terminal
HILTON AUCKLAND
Queens Wharf
Bledisloe Terminal
Captain Cook Wharf
Marsden Wharf
Bledisloe Wharf
Jellicoe Wharf

America's Cup Village
Auckland Fish Market
Hobson Wharf
National Maritime Museum
Ferry Berth
Ferry Building

St Joseph Home

Shelly Beach

Ponsonby Intermediate School
Pompallier Terrace

Gas Works
St Marys College
Victoria Park
College Hill

Auckland Mail Service Centre
Victoria West
Victoria Park Market
THE HERITAGE AUCKLAND
St Patricks
St Matthews
Television Centre
SKY CITY GRAND
Sky Tower and Casino
Civic Theatre
Art Gallery

SEBEL
Quay
CORTHORNE
Britomart Transport Centre
Customs East
Quay
STAMFORD PLAZA
MERCURE HOTEL WINDSOR
Fort
Shortland
ASCOTT METROPOLIS
ASPEN HOUSE
HYATT REGENCY
Chancery
Waterloo Quadrant
Albert Park
Auckland University
St Andrews

Vector Arena
Former Auckland Railway Station
The Strand

Ponsonby
School
Ponsonby 24hr Medical Centre

Freemans Bay School
Freemans Bay
Western Park
Auckland Girls Grammar School

Aotea Centre
Town Hall
Methodist Mission
RENDEZVOUS AUCKLAND
Myers Park
PARK TOWERS
Auckland University of Technology

Auckland University
Parnell

Auckland City

Carlaw Park
Lower Domain

Auckland Domain

Grey Lynn
Grey Lynn Park

Salvation Army
Newton
Karangahape
Hopetoun
Auckland Hebrew Congregation
LANGHAM AUCKLAND

Arch Hill

North Western Motorway
AUCKLAND ZOO
Nixon Park

Ian McKinnon Drive
Newton
Grafton
Khyber Pass
St Benedicts

Grafton Bridge
Grafton

St Peters College
Khyber Pass

Winter Gardens
Auckland War Memorial Museum
Maunsell

School of Medicine
Carlton Gore
Carlton Gore

Kingsland
Kowhai Intermediate School

Eden Terrace
Mt Eden Railway Station
Edenvale Cres
EDEN LODGE

Mt Eden Prison
Auckland Grammar School

Newmarket
Newmarket Station
Auckland Surgical Clinic

Eden Park

Mt Eden School

Mt Eden
Mt Eden Domain
Mt Eden

Mercy
Omana
Withiel Thomas Park
Glenfell Place

Epsom
Epsom Girls Grammar School

Morningside

Auckland Hamilton (Southern Motorway)

Northland

Northland consists of a 350km-long peninsula, beginning at the town of Warkworth and extending northwest to North Cape. In Maori legend the great Polynesian voyagers discovered the Hokianga Harbour in about 1100AD. Settlement followed, early Maori finding Northland's subtropical climate, the many harbours and an abundance of fish and birds ideal for their way of life. The region has two coasts which are distinctly different. The west coast is almost straight and buffeted by strong, wind-driven waves; the east coast is relatively sheltered, with many beautiful bays, secluded coves, islands and white sand beaches.

MAIN ATTRACTIONS

- **Cape Reinga**, which in Maori legend is the departing place of the spirits of the dead. Just off the cape is the turbulent meeting place of two great bodies of water, the Tasman Sea and the Pacific Ocean.
- The **Waipoua Forest** and **Trounson Kauri Park** near the west coast of Northland, where New Zealand's largest surviving **kauri trees** can be seen. These include **Tane Mahuta** ('Lord of the Forest'), the mightiest kauri of all, which is estimated to be between 1500 and 2000 years old.
- The **mountainous golden sand dunes** at the mouth of the **Hokianga Harbour** and at **Te Paki**, on the west coast of the Far North, which are great for **sand-boarding**.

- The **Bay of Islands** is an essential Northland attraction (*see* p. 13).
- **Diving** around the **Poor Knights Islands Marine Reserve**, off the east coast at Whananaki, New Zealand's most notable dive site.
- The **Kauri Museum**, Church Road, Matakohe. Its dramatic displays show how the felling, transportation and milling of kauri trees defined the colonial history of Northland and nearby **Kaipara Harbour** for several decades. Another valuable industry was digging for fossilized kauri gum, in northern swamplands.
- A coach tour from Kaitaia along **Ninety Mile Beach**, home of the endangered shellfish delicacy, the burrowing toheroa.

USEFUL CONTACTS

Destination Northland, Level 2, The Mall, Marsden Rd, Paihia, Bay of Islands, tel: (09) 402 7683, fax: (09) 402 7672, e-mail: info@northlandnz.com website: www.northlandnz.com
The **Far North i-SITE Visitor Centre**: South Road, Kaitaia, tel: (09) 408 0879, website: www.topofnz.co.nz
Whangarei i-SITE Visitor Centre: 92 Otaika Road, Whangarei, tel: (09) 438 1079, website: www.northlandnz.com

Opposite: *An aerial view of Moturua Island, Bay of Islands, revealing the bay's clear waters, sheltered anchorages and white sand beaches.*
Below: *The lighthouse at Cape Reinga, Northland. The cape marks the meeting place of the Tasman Sea and the Pacific Ocean.*

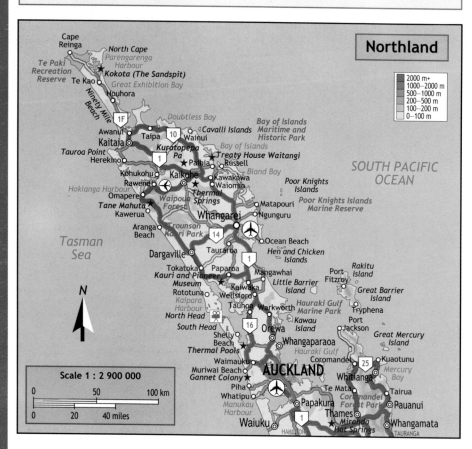

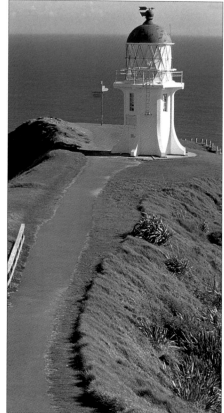

Bay of Islands

The Bay of Islands, on the east coast of Northland, is one of New Zealand's pre-eminent visitor attractions. It consists of an extensive complex of peaceful beaches, peninsulas, capes, bays and over 150 islands, all within easy reach of the area's two main towns, Paihia and Russell. The bay is renowned for its fishing, fertile lowlands and sheltered beaches, making it a densely populated district for local Maori at the time of first European contact. New Zealand's first capital, Kororareka, a lawless town in the 1820s and 30s, was built on the site of present-day Russell. Today the harbourfront town is one of the most historic and attractive in New Zealand.

MAIN ATTRACTIONS

- The **Treaty House,** home of the early British resident, James Busby, and site of the signing of the Treaty of Waitangi on 6 February 1840.
- A cruise in a catamaran to **Cape Brett** and the **Hole in the Rock**.
- **Swimming with dolphins** in the bay.
- The beautiful waterfront town of Russell has a number of historical buildings. This town is also the head quarters of the **Bay of Islands game-fishing industry.**
- **Te Waimate Mission House** (1832), Waimate North, Whangarei. A preserved, deeply significant historic house where the second signing of the **Treaty of Waitangi** occurred.
- A **game-fishing excursion** on a launch which can be chartered from the Russell waterfront. Game fish taken include marlin, tuna, shark and kingfish.
- **Scuba diving** at the **Poor Knights Islands,** known as one of the world's top ten dives.

USEFUL CONTACTS

Russell is best approached by vehicle ferry from the little port of Opua. The ferry trip takes ten minutes, followed by a ten-minute drive to the town. Paihia and Russell, which face each other across the bay, are also connected by a passenger ferry service.
Bay of Islands i-SITE Visitor Centre: The Wharf, Marsden Road, Paihia, tel: (09) 402 7345, e-mail: visitorinfo@fndc.govt.nz website: www.fndc.govt.nz/infocentre
Destination Northland: Level 2, The Mall, Marsden Road, Paihia, tel: (09) 402 7683, website: www.northlandnz.com
Tai Tokerau Tourism: website: www.taitokerau.co.nz

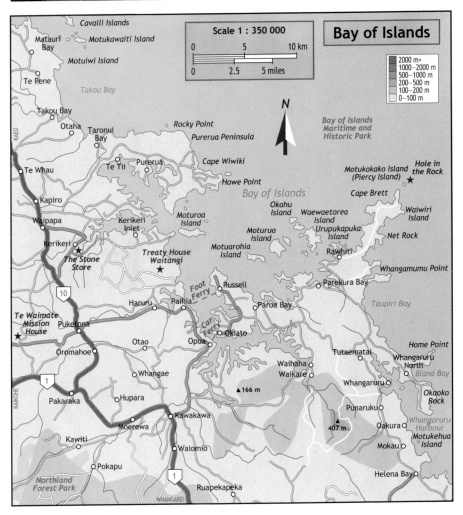

Coromandel

The Coromandel is a mountainous, forested peninsula lined on both coasts by beautiful beaches, sheltered bays and estuaries. In the 19th century the area was milled ruthlessly for kauri timber and mined for quartz gold, which ravaged the natural landscape, but today the peninsula has recovered and is home to many environmentalists, artists and craftspeople. The Coromandel is a popular holiday region for people from Auckland and Hamilton — both two hours' drive away — as well as having a sizeable permanent population. Roads follow both the west and east coasts, while it is also possible to drive across the rugged peninsula.

ACCOMMODATION

Star and Garter Hotel:
5 Kapanga Road, Coromandel town,
tel/fax: (07) 866 8160,
e-mail: karen@starandgarter.co.nz
website: www.starandgarter.co.nz
A centrally located historic hotel.

Rapaura Water Gardens:
586 Tapu-Coroglen Road, Tapu,
Thames Coast, tel/fax: (07) 868 4821,
e-mail: rapaura.watergardens@xtra.
co.nz website: www.rapaurawater
gardens.co.nz Self-catering accommodation, set among beautifully landscaped gardens and forest, in the
midst of the Coromandel Forest Park.

Tatahi Lodge: 9 Grange Road, Hahei,
tel: (07) 866 3992, fax: (07) 866 3993,
e-mail: tatahi_lodge@xtra.co.nz
website: www.dreamland.co.nz/
tatahilodge Motel units and a back-
packers' lodge in a tranquil setting,
just a stroll from Hahei Beach and the
settlement's cafés and shops.

Opposite: *White Island, an active volcano in the Bay of Plenty.*
Below: *Kayaking on Tairua Harbour. In the background is Paku Peak.*

MAIN ATTRACTIONS

- The **east coast beaches**, especially Hot Water Beach, Hahei, Tairua and Whangamata.
- The many **hiking trails** through **Coromandel Forest Park**, such as the **Kauaeranga Valley Kauri Trail**.
- Amazing views from **Paku**, a **volcanic peak** overlooking the **Tairua estuary** and **Pauanui Beach**.
- The walk to beautiful **Cathedral Cove** from Hahei beach.
- A ride on the narrow-gauge line through regenerating native forest at **Driving Creek**, above **Coromandel** town.
- **Sea kayaking** along the coast between Hahei and Hot Water Beach.
- A **scenic drive** on SH25, the 309 Road or the Tapu-Coroglen Road.
- A visit to the **Thames School of Mines and Mineralogical Museum**, in Thames, to see the impact of 19th-century gold-mining on the region.

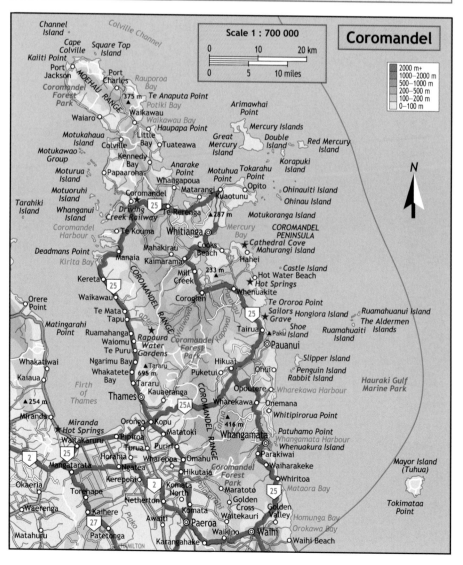

Coastal Bay of Plenty

The Bay of Plenty, named thus by Captain James Cook in 1769, is a fitting description. The region possesses fertile soils, high sunshine hours and mild temperatures and an arc of sheltered coastal lowland where agricultural production is intensive. Much of the plain formerly used for pastoral farming has been converted to horticulture, producing crops such as kiwifruit, avocadoes, tamarillos, mandarins, grapes and other exotic crops. The region's city, Tauranga, is one of New Zealand's fastest-growing centres. Its port is busy exporting the commodities of the region, including forest products and horticultural crops.

MAIN ATTRACTIONS

- **Body surfing** and **board-riding** at the beach at Mount Maunganui.
- A **hike** to the summit of Mauao (232m), at **Mount Maunganui**.
- A **helicopter flight** out to the crater of the Bay of Plenty's **live volcano, White Island**.
- **Game-fishing** in the waters around **Mayor Island**.
- A visit to **Kiwi360**, 81 Young Road, Te Puke, to learn all about the region's best-known product, **kiwifruit**.
- **White-water rafting** down one of the rivers which descend from the **Kaimai Ranges**.
- Sampling the region's fine food and wines at one of **Tauranga harbour's** restaurants.
- A visit to a **winery**, for wine tasting and gate sales.
- A **coastal drive** to the eastern Bay of Plenty, to visit the river-mouth town of **Whakatane** and the beach at **Ohope**, one of New Zealand's best.

USEFUL CONTACTS

Tauranga i-SITE: 95 Willow Street, Tauranga, tel: (07) 578 8103, e-mail: trgvin@tauranga.govt.nz

Mount Maunganui i-SITE: Salisbury Avenue, Mount Maunganui, tel: (07) 575 5099, e-mail: trgvin@tauranga.govt.nz

ACCOMMODATION

Hotel on Devonport: 72 Devonport Road, Tauranga, tel: (07) 578 2668, fax: (07) 578 2669, freephone 0800 322 856, e-mail: reservations@hotelondevonport.net.nz website: www.hotel ondevonport.net.nz A luxurious boutique hotel in central Tauranga.

Kingsview Resort: 6 Durham Street, Tauranga, tel: (07) 571 1455, fax: (07) 571 1456, freephone: 0800 805 464, e-mail: info@kingsviewresort.co.nz

website: www.kingsviewresort.co.nz A newish resort, right in the heart of Tauranga.

Oceanside Twin Towers Resort: 1 Maunganui Road, Mount Maunganui, tel: (07) 575 5371, freephone 0800 466 868, e-mail: info@oceanside.co.nz website: www.oceanside.co.nz Beachside accommodation at 'the Mount', opposite one of New Zealand's finest swimming and surfing beaches.

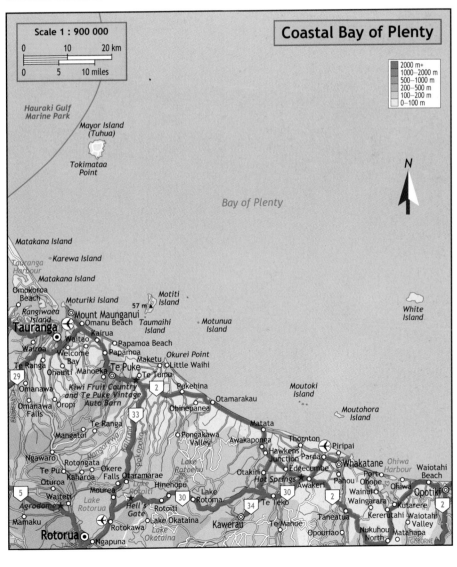

Coastal Bay of Plenty

Rotorua Region

The Rotorua region is one of New Zealand's leading tourist destinations, with many unique natural attractions. The area lies directly across a zone of intense active volcanism, and since Victorian times visitors have been spellbound by the region's dramatic geothermal activities, which include steaming, silica-encrusted lakes, boiling mud pools, belching geysers and explosive volcanic vents. 'Taking the waters' in the region's naturally heated mineral pools has been a popular diversion from colonial times until the present day. The Rotorua region has been home to the Arawa tribe of the Maori people since about the 14th century.

TRAVEL TIPS

i-SITE Visitor Information: cnr Fenton and Haupapa Streets, Rotorua, tel: (07) 348 5179, fax: (07) 348 6044, website: www.rotoruaNZ.com You will find information and bookings for accommodation, Maori 'hangi' and concerts, sightseeing and adventure tours. Examples of the region's thermal attractions can be seen at www.geyserland.co.nz

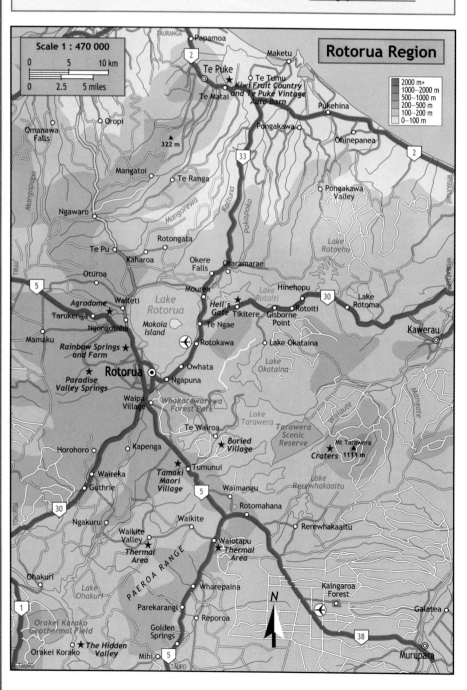

MAIN ATTRACTIONS

- The village of Te Wairoa, Rotorua's Pompeii, which was buried by the eruption of Mount Tarawera in 1886.
- **The Hidden Valley**, Orakei Korako, an unspoilt thermal reserve of geysers, mud pools and silica terraces, 45 minutes south of Rotorua.
- **Hell's Gate**, or **Tikitere**, a thermal wonderland, northeast of Rotorua.
- The crystalline streams and trout pools at **Rainbow Springs**, 4km northwest of Rotorua.
- The farm animal activities at the **Agrodome**, 5km northwest of Rotorua.
- **Trout fishing** on one of the region's many lakes or rivers.
- **White-water rafting** on one of the region's cascading rivers, such as the **Kaituna**.
- An excursion to the crater of **Mount Tarawera**, the source of the great eruption of 1886.

Central Rotorua

Rotorua means 'Two lakes', a reference to the fact that the city lies on the southern shore of Lake Rotorua, which is joined by a narrow channel to a second lake, Rotoiti, to the northeast. Rotorua town first began at Ohinemutu, on the lakefront half a kilometre northwest of the present city centre, where there are hot springs for cooking and bathing. From above the city Rotorua appears swathed in steam as superheated water escapes from hundreds of vents in the earth's crust. Nicknamed 'Sulphur City' because of the smell of hydrogen sulphide given off from these vents, Rotorua maintains a thriving tourist industry based on its unique geothermal landscapes.

MAIN ATTRACTIONS

- The gardens, steam vents and Tudor-style building in the **Government Gardens**, in central Rotorua. The building also houses the **Museum of Art and History**.
- **Polynesian Spa**, Hinemoa Street, Rotorua. A complex of hot mineral pools and spa therapies.
- **Historic St Faith's Anglican church**, on the shores of Lake Rotorua at Ohinemutu. The church features beautifully carved panels, called in Maori 'tukutuku'.
- The geysers, mud pools and Maori village of **Whakarewarewa Thermal Reserve**.
- A launch trip out to the legendary island, **Mokoia**, in Lake Rotorua.
- An evening of traditional Maori **singing and dancing**, accompanied by food cooked in a 'hangi' (earth oven).

Opposite: *The Champagne thermal pool at Waiotapu, Rotorua region.*
Below: *Government Gardens and Rotorua Museum, a short walk from the city centre. In the gardens are several active volcanic vents.*

ACCOMMODATION

Four Canoes Hotel: 273 Fenton Street, Rotorua, tel: (07) 348 9184, fax: (07) 348 6144, e-mail: reservations@fourcanoes.com website: www.fourcanoes.com A boutique hotel inspired by Maori culture.
Millennium Hotel Rotorua: corner Eruera and Hinemaru Streets, Rotorua, tel: (07) 347 1234, fax: (07) 348 1234, e-mail: millennium.rotorua@mckhotels.co.nz website: www.millenniumrotorua.co.nz

Deluxe accommodation, within an easy walk from Lake Rotorua and the Polynesian Spa, with in-house massages and beauty therapies also available.
The Princes Gate Hotel: 1057 Arawa Street, Rotorua, tel: (07) 348 1179, fax: (07) 348 6215, e-mail: princes.gate@clear.net.nz website: www.princesgate.co.nz An historic hotel, directly opposite the Government Gardens.

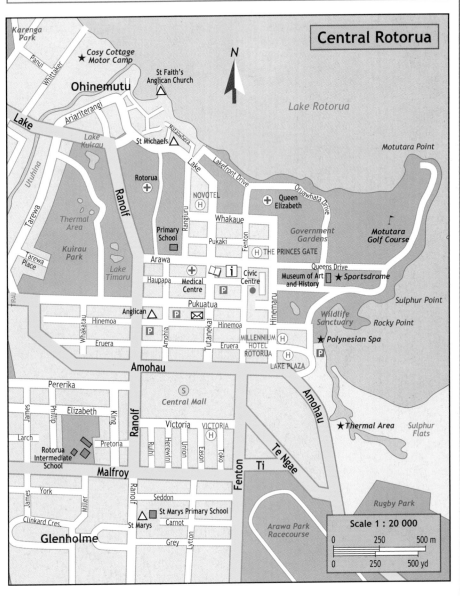

Central Rotorua

Taupo

'Taupo' is the name for New Zealand's largest lake and the resort town which lies at its northern end. Lake Taupo occupies a vast depression in the centre of the North Island, 355—357m above sea level. The depression was created by a titanic volcanic explosion in the year 186AD. Later the depression filled with water from rivers and streams, creating a lake 616km² in size. New Zealand's longest river, the Waikato, flows from the lake's northern end. Late in the 19th century rainbow and brown trout were introduced to the lake and its tributary rivers from North America. The trout thrived and led to Lake Taupo and the rivers becoming world famous for their angling.

ACCOMMODATION

The Point Villas: 24 The Point, Acacia Bay Road, PO Box 1635, Taupo, tel: (07) 579 2731, fax: (07) 579 2732, e-mail: relax@thepointvillas.co.nz website: www.thepointvillas.co.nz Beautiful villas in a secluded estate setting; only a 10-minute drive from Taupo town.

Bayview Wairakei Resort: 9km north of Taupo town on SH1, freephone: 0800 737 678, e-mail: stay@wairakei.co.nz website: www.wairakei.co.nz A resort located in Wairakei Thermal Valley.

Lake Taupo Lodge: 41 Mapara Road, Acacia Bay, tel: (07) 378 7386, fax: (07) 377 3226, e-mail: reservations@laketaupolodge.co.nz website: www.laketaupolodge.co.nz A lodge set among landscaped gardens, overlooking Lake Taupo.

The Cove: 213 Lake Terrace, Taupo, tel: (07) 378 7599, fax: (07) 378 7393, e-mail: stay@thecove.co.nz website: www.thecove.co.nz Intimate, boutique accommodation with a lakeside restaurant.

Te Kowhai Landing: 325 Lake Terrace, 2 Mile Bay, Taupo, freephone: 0800 377 3623, fax: (07) 574 8096, e-mail: stay@essencenz.com website: www.essencenz.com This establishment consists of self-contained, lake-edge units.

TRAVEL TIPS

- Website: www.laketauponz.com
- **Taupo i-SITE Visitor Centre:** 30 Tongariro St, Taupo, tel: (07) 376 0027.
- **Turangi i-SITE Visitor Centre:** Ngawaka Place, Turangi, tel: (07) 386 8999, fax: (07) 386 0074, e-mail: turangivc@laketauponz.com
- **Ruapehu i-SITE Visitor Centre:** 54 Clyde St, Ohakune, tel: (06) 385 8427, www.visitruapehu.co.nz

MAIN ATTRACTIONS

- Walking around the northern shore of **Lake Taupo** on a **public walkway**.
- **Trout fishing** on Lake Taupo and its tributary rivers.
- **Swimming**, **sailing**, **kayaking** and **water-skiing** on Lake Taupo.
- **Huka Falls**, just north of Taupo, where the Waikato River pours through a narrow chasm.
- **Jet boating** on the Waikato River, right up to the base of Huka Falls.
- The drive down the eastern side of Lake Taupo, which follows the shores of the lake to the **Tongariro River**.
- Relaxing in a **hot pool** at one of the district's **spas** or **thermal parks**.
- **Shopping** for souvenirs in Taupo town's many **boutiques** and **shops**.

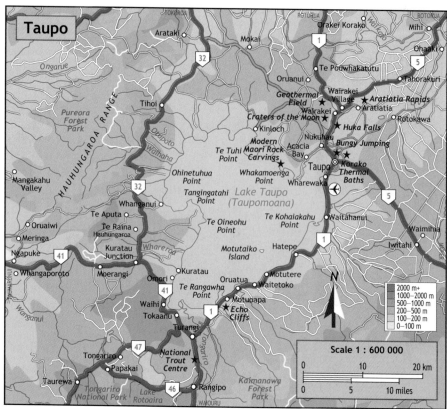

Central Plateau

The central plateau is the roof of New Zealand's North Island. It consists of a trio of active volcanoes: Mount Ruapehu (2797m), Mount Ngauruhoe (2291m) and Mount Tongariro (1967m). These mountains comprise the core of Tongariro National Park, a unique wilderness region of active volcanoes, tussock grasslands, hot springs, lakes and lava formations. Many of the Lord of the Rings scenes were shot in this area. In summer the park's tramping tracks attract thousands of hikers, in winter it is the North Island's premier ski region. Mount Ruapehu has two large skifields on its western slopes and one smaller field on its eastern side.

Above: *Tama Lakes, volcanic craters along the Tongariro Crossing.*
Opposite: *Huka Falls, Waikato River.*
Below: *Mount Ruapehu, at 2797m, is the North Island's highest mountain and an active volcano.*

MAIN ATTRACTIONS

- **The Tongariro Crossing**, a hiking trail which winds through the centre of the region's volcanic landscape.
- **Skiing** on Turoa and Whakapapa fields, on Mount Ruapehu.
- The drive across the **Desert Road** from Turangi to Waiouru, the North Island's only cold desert.
- An evening of fine dining at the **Bayview Chateau Tongariro**, an elegant historic hotel on the slopes of Mount Ruapehu.
- Visiting the **Tongariro National Trout Centre**, State Highway 1, just south of Turangi, to see wild and tame trout and displays of the species' life cycle.

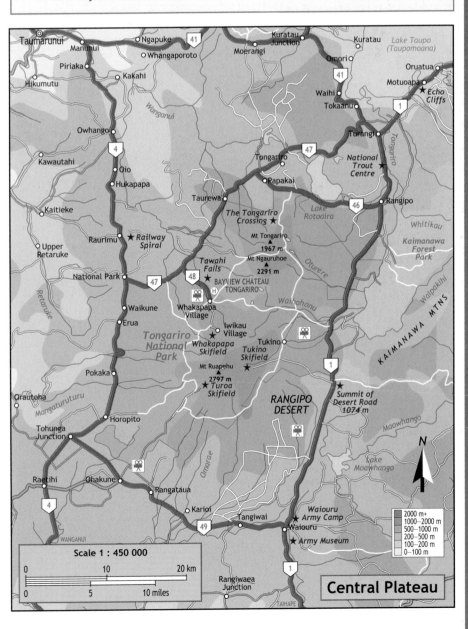

Central Plateau

Scale 1 : 450 000

Napier

Napier sits on the edge of the fertile Hawke's Bay lowland. In 1931 Napier and its neighbouring city, Hastings, suffered great damage when the bay was struck by an earthquake measuring 7.8 on the Richter scale, killing 256 people in the Hawke's Bay region. After the earthquake an expanse of land behind the city was raised from the sea. Napier's airport, some farmland and the western suburbs of the city occupy this 'new land' today. Napier was then rebuilt in the prevailing Art Deco style of the early 1930s, and so today the city boasts one of the largest collections of this style of architecture in the world.

USEFUL CONTACTS

Napier i-SITE Visitor Centre:
100 Marine Parade, Napier,
tel: (06) 834 1911 or 0800 429 537,
e-mail: info@napiervic.co.nz
websites: www.hawkesbaynz.com
www.isitehawkesbay.co.nz
www.artdeconapier.com

MAIN ATTRACTIONS

- The view of **Napier city** and **Hawke's Bay** from the summit of Bluff Hill (102m) above the town.
- A self-guided walk through Napier and along **Marine Parade**, to savour the Art Deco buildings of the city.
- Visit the **Hawke's Bay Museum**, on Marine Parade, to experience the history of Napier and its region.
- Souvenir shopping at **Napier's Art Deco Shop** in Tennyson Street.

Left: The Napier Dome, one of the many Art Deco buildings of the city.

ACCOMMODATION

The County Hotel: 12 Browning Street, Napier, tel: (06) 835 7800, fax: (06) 835 7797, e-mail: countyhotel@xtra.co.nz website: www.countyhotel.co.nz
Luxury accommodation with an award-winning restaurant, Chambers.
Scenic Circle Te Pania Hotel: 45 Marine Parade, Napier, tel: (06) 833 7733, fax: (06) 833 7732, e-mail: te.pania@ scenic-circle.co.nz website: www. scenic-circle.co.nz Studio-style rooms right on the waterfront.
Ormlie Lodge: Omarunui Road, Taradale, Napier. tel: (06) 844 5774, fax: (06) 844 5499,
website: www.ormlielodge.com
A historic country manor house.
Breckenridge Lodge: 1 Breckenridge Lane, Taradale, tel: (06) 844 9411, fax: (06) 844 9411, website: www.brecken ridgelodge.co.nz Set among vineyards.

Hawke's Bay

Hawke's Bay consists of a long, picturesque coastline and a sheltered, fertile lowland. Known as 'the Fruitbowl of New Zealand', Hawke's Bay is a very productive horticultural region, based on its fertile alluvial soils and high sunshine hours. The bay itself, called Hawke Bay, is bounded by two large promontories, Mahia Peninsula to the north and Cape Kidnappers to the south. The agricultural districts surrounding Napier and Hastings are noted for their orchards, vineyards, wineries and fine wines, particularly pinot noir, chardonnay, cabernet sauvignon and sauvignon blanc.

MAIN ATTRACTIONS

- The views over Hawke's Bay from **Te Mata Peak** (399m), east of Hastings.
- A visit to **Cape Kidnappers**, the world's largest, most accessible mainland gannet colony.
- A tour of the region along some of its many **food and wine trails**.
- Self-drive or walk one of the region's **17 heritage trails**.
- Visit the area's traditional **farmers' markets**, to shop for the freshest local produce and organic foods.
- Rise early for a **hot-air balloon ride** and aerial views of the Heretaunga Plains.

Above: Views over Napier city and the Hawke's Bay coast from Bluff Hill, in the northeast of the city.

USEFUL CONTACTS

Hawke's Bay:
Website: www.hawkesbaynz.com
Freephone: 0800 HAWKES (0800 429 537)
Hastings i-SITE Visitor Centre:
Westerman's Building, cnr Russell & Heretaunga St East, Hastings, freephone: 0800 HASTINGS (0800 4278 4647), tel: (06) 873 0080, e-mail: vic@hastingstourism.co.nz
website: www.hastings.co.nz
Havelock North Village Info:
At the Roundabout, Havelock North, tel: (06) 877 9600, e-mail: info@villageinfo.co.nz
Art Deco weekend:
Held in the third week of February.
Websites: www.artdeconapier.com and www.hawkesbaynz.com/events

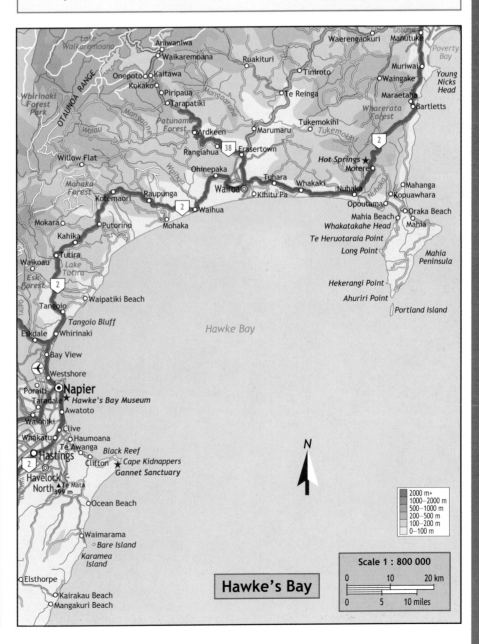

Hawke's Bay

Scale 1 : 800 000

Central Wellington

Wellington city, the capital of New Zealand since 1865, is defined geographically by its superb harbour. The town was founded in 1840 and grew around the harbour shores and up the steep hills that surround it on all sides. Today it is a very compact city, with most public amenities within walking distance of one another. Many steep steps and paths pass from the city's central business district and up to the houses on the hills, providing panoramic harbour views along the way. New Zealand's parliament and the government's administrative buildings are located in Thorndon, at the northern end of Lambton Quay, near the central city.

ACCOMMODATION

Duxton Hotel, 170 Wakefield Street, freephone: 0800 655 555, tel: (04) 473 3900, fax: (04) 473 3929, e-mail: res@wellington.duxton.co.nz website: www.duxton.com Located centrally between the city's main shopping and entertainment districts.
Portland Hotel, 24 Hawkestone Street, Thorndon, tel: (04) 473 2208, fax: (04) 473 3892, e-mail: enquiries@portlandhotel.co.nz website: www.portlandhotel.co.nz Near train/bus/ferry terminals and Westpac Trust Stadium.
Central City Apartment Hotel: 130 Victoria Street, tel: (04) 385 4166, fax: (04) 385 4167, e-mail: reservations@ccah.co.nz website: www.centralcityhotel.co.nz Studio apartments right in the heart of the city's shopping districts.
Museum Hotel, 90 Cable Street, tel: (04) 802 8900, freephone: 0800 994 335, fax: (04) 802 8909, e-mail: info@museumhotel.co.nz website: www.museumhotel.co.nz

Left: *Chaffers Marina is at Oriental Bay, central Wellington.*
Below: *Wellington city's cable car.*

MAIN ATTRACTIONS

- A trip on the **cable car**, from **Lambton Quay** to the **Botanic Gardens**, making three stops along the way. The views from the top are superb.
- **Museum of Wellington City and Sea**, Queens Wharf. The museum explores Wellington's unique character, from first settlement by Maori and Europeans.
- **Museum of New Zealand — Te Papa Tongarewa**, a five-storey complex of exhibitions depicting New Zealand's history, landscapes and different cultures.
- **The Karori Wildlife Sanctuary**, end of Waiapu Road, Karori. A reserve enclosed by a predator-proof fence, only minutes' drive from the city centre, where native **fauna and flora** can be seen thriving.
- A one-hour, free guided tour of New Zealand's **parliament buildings**, in Thorndon.
- The walk around the **waterfront** to sheltered **Oriental Bay**, a strip of golden sand from where there are broad views of the **harbour** and the central business district.
- **Dining** at one of the many cafés and restaurants in **Courtenay Place**, at the southern end of the central business district.
- An excursion across the harbour by ferry to **Days Bays** for a café lunch and a walk on the beach.

Central Wellington

Scale 1 : 12 500

0   125   250 m

0   125   250 yd

Nelson Region

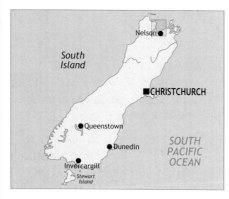

Nelson is the geographic centre of New Zealand and the principal city of the northern region of the South Island. Located on the eastern shores of Tasman Bay, Nelson is surrounded by the Richmond and Arthur Ranges, which shelter the city from the prevailing winds and make the region one of the sunniest in New Zealand. The Tasman Bay lowland, behind Nelson, is a very productive horticultural area and the city's port is an export outlet for fruit, timber, forest products and fish. The Nelson region is also notable for the number of artisans it supports, particularly potters, ceramicists and glass artists.

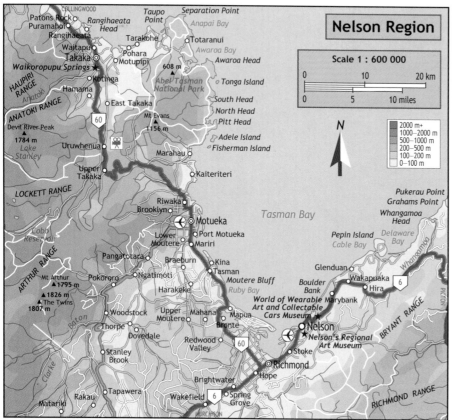

MAIN ATTRACTIONS

- The Saturday morning **market** in **Montgomery Square**, Nelson, when dozens of stalls display the goods the region is noted for, especially **arts and crafts**.
- The **cafés and restaurants** along **Wakefield Quay**, Nelson.
- The **World of Wearable Art and Collectable Cars Museum**, Nelson.
- **Nelson's regional art museum**, The Suter Te Aratoi o Whakatu.
- One of Nelson's **art and sculpture walks** through the city and along the waterfront.
- The sand **beaches** at Kaiteriteri.
- **Hiking** and **sea kayaking** in **Abel Tasman National Park**.
- Springs and scenic walks at Waikoropupu Springs.

ACCOMMODATION

Wakefield Quay House, 385 Wakefield Quay, Port Hills, Nelson, tel: (03) 546 7275, e-mail: wakefieldquay@xtra.co.nz website: www.wakefieldquay.co.nz A restored colonial villa with glorious harbour views.
Copthorne Rutherford, Trafalgar Square, Nelson, tel: (03) 548 2299, fax: (03) 546 3003, e-mail: enquiries@rutherfordhotel.co.nz website: www.rutherfordhotel.co.nz A quality hotel, centrally located.
Cathedral Inn Bed and Breakfast, 369 Trafalgar Street South, Nelson, tel: (03) 548 7369, fax: (03) 548 0369, e-mail: enquiries@cathedralinn.co.nz website: www.cathedralinn.co.nz A fully refurbished historic home.
Nelson motel accommodation: tel: (03) 546 5070 or visit the website: www.nelsonmotels.co.nz

Left: *Kaiteriteri beach, Motueka district, west of Nelson.*

Marlborough Region

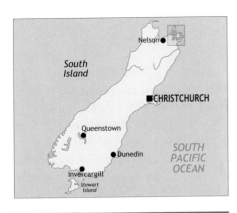

Marlborough, which occupies the northeastern corner of the South Island, is a region of picturesque sounds — 'drowned' sea valleys — the Richmond mountain range and a broad river valley, the Wairau. The valley comprises New Zealand's largest grape-growing region, based on its alluvial soils and the highest sunshine hours in the country. Some eighty Marlborough wineries produce 40% of New Zealand's output, mainly sauvignon blanc. The Wairau River flows into Cloudy Bay, which is also the name of the region's best-known white wine. The two towns which serve the Marlborough region are Picton and Blenheim.

ACCOMMODATION

Old Saint Mary's Convent Retreat, 776 Rapaura Road, RD3, Blenheim, tel: (03) 570 5700, fax: (03) 570 5703, e-mail: retreat@convent.co.nz website: www.convent.co.nz Historic property featuring native timbers.
Vintner's Retreat, 55 Rapaura Road, Blenheim, tel: (03) 572 7420, fax: (03) 572 7421, freephone: 0800 484 686, e-mail: info@vintnersrestreat.co.nz website: www.vintnersrestreat.co.nz European-style accommodation in the midst of a vineyard.
Chateau Marlborough, cnr High and Henry Streets, Blenheim, freephone: 0800 752 275, tel: (03) 578 0064, fax: (03) 578 2661, e-mail: chateau@marlboroughnz.co.nz website: www.marlboroughnz.co.nz Self-catering studio units, two minutes' walk from the town centre.

USEFUL CONTACTS

Nelson i-SITE Visitor Centre, Millars Acre Centre, 77 Trafalgar Street, Nelson, tel: (03) 548 2304, fax: (03) 546 7393, e-mail: vin@nelsonNZ.com website: www.nelsonNZ.com
Golden Bay i-SITE Visitor Centre, Willow Street, Takaka, tel: (03) 525 9136, fax: (03) 525 9288, e-mail: gb.vin@nelsonNZ.com website: www.nelsonNZ.com
Blenheim i-SITE Visitor Centre, Blenheim Railway Station, SH1, Blenheim, tel: (03) 577 8080, fax: (03) 577 8079, e-mail: blenheim@i-site.org
Picton i-SITE Visitor Centre, Picton Foreshore, tel: (03) 520 3113, fax: (03) 573 5021, e-mail: picton@i-SITE.org
Marlborough tourism website: www.destinationmarlborough.com

Above: *Vineyard on the Wairau Plain, Marlborough.*

MAIN ATTRACTIONS

- Touring the **Marlborough vineyards and wineries**.
- **Hiking** along the **Queen Charlotte Track**.
- Having a meal of mussels at **Havelock**, the greenshell mussel capital of the world.
- Taking the **scenic drive** from **Picton** to **Havelock** to **Nelson**.
- Cruising the waterways of the **Marlborough Sounds**.
- Following the **Arts and Craft Trail** from the Awatere River to the Marlborough Sounds.

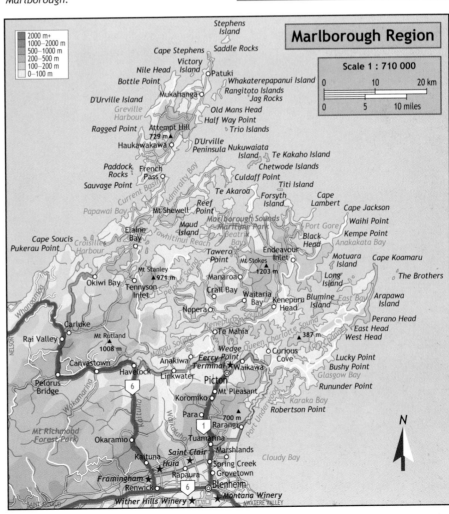

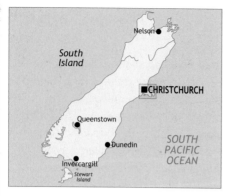

Christchurch Region

The Canterbury Plains comprise New Zealand's most extensive lowland region. The plains were built up over millions of years from alluvial material eroded from the valleys of the Southern Alps and deposited in the sea by several large 'braided' rivers which flow down from the Alps. The plains eventually became joined to an extinct volcano lying off the east coast, which is now called Banks Peninsula. Christchurch, the South Island's largest commercial and industrial centre, lies on the eastern edge of the Canterbury Plains. Founded in the 1840s, Christchurch's central streets are set out in a grid pattern around Cathedral Square.

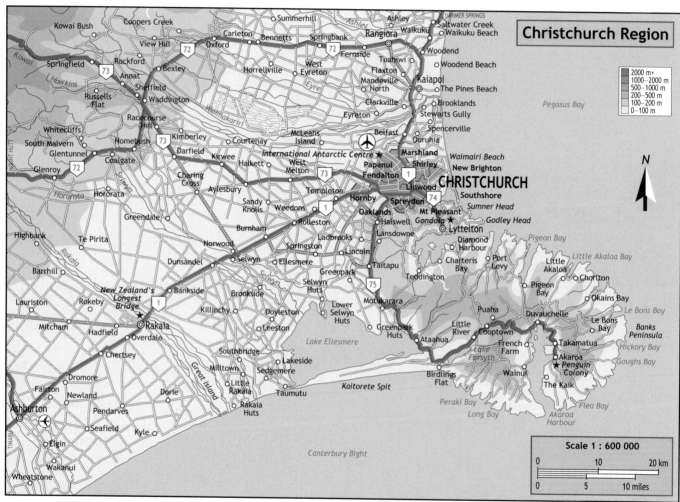

MAIN ATTRACTIONS

- **Hiking** to and from Akaroa, with its French colonial history, to experience the rugged scenery along the walkway on Banks Peninsula.
- Lunching in the historic **Hurunui Hotel**.
- Swimming with **Hector's dolphins**, the world's rarest dolphins, in Akaroa Harbour.
- **Skiing** at the Mount Hutt or Porter Heights skifields.
- Shopping at the quality shops and galleries in **The Arts Centre**, in Worcester Boulevard, Christchurch.
- **Dining** at one of the many ethnic restaurants in central Christchurch.
- Exploring the past at the **Canterbury Museum** in Christchurch.
- Jogging, cycling or walking in **Hagley Park**, Christchurch.
- **Punting** on the River Avon.
- Riding on the **tram** around central Christchurch, following the 'City Loop'.
- Taking the Christchurch **gondola** to the top of Mount Pleasant.
- Visiting the **International Antarctic Centre**, near Christchurch Airport.

Central Christchurch

Christchurch lies to the west of Banks Peninsula, and spreads northeast to the coast at New Brighton and southeast to the Port Hills. A road tunnel through the Port Hills leads to the city's port, Lyttelton. Central Christchurch retains a very 'English' atmosphere, with its many stone neo-Gothic buildings, the meandering Avon River and extensive gardens and parks, the largest of which is Hagley Park. Large numbers of deciduous trees in the parks are a reminder of the city's English founders. The central city's streets lead to the Square and its Cathedral, which was modelled on Caen Cathedral in Normandy. The city's tourist attractions include Hagley Park, where there are walking paths, a golf course and the city's Botanic Garden. A short walk away in Worcester Boulevard is the Arts Centre, located in neo-Gothic buildings which once accommodated the University of Canterbury. Here there are now art and craft stalls, art galleries, boutiques and a theatre of performing arts.

ACCOMMODATION

Heritage Christchurch, 28-30 Cathedral Square, tel: (03) 377 9722, fax: (03) 377 9881, e-mail: res@heritagehotels.co.nz website: www.heritagehotels.co.nz A refurbished historic building.

Chateau Blanc Suites, Cranmer Square (cnr Montreal & Kilmore Sts), freephone: 0800 784 837, tel: (03) 365 1600, fax: (03) 353 0974, e-mail: suites@chateaublanc.co.nz website: www.chateaublanc.co.nz Apartments with kitchens and balconies, five minutes from the city centre.

Warners Historic Hotel, 50 Cathedral Square, tel: (03) 366 5159, fax: (03) 397 5736, e-mail: reception@warnershotel.co.nz website: www.warnershotel.co.nz Established in 1863 and thoroughly modernized, this hotel is located in the heart of the city.

Opposite: *The City Loop Tram on New Regent Street, central Christchurch.*
Below: *Chalice, a 21st-century sculpture, with Christchurch Cathedral behind.*

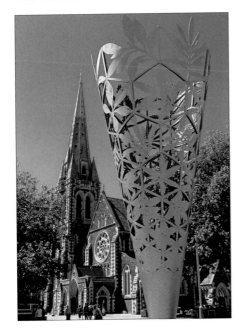

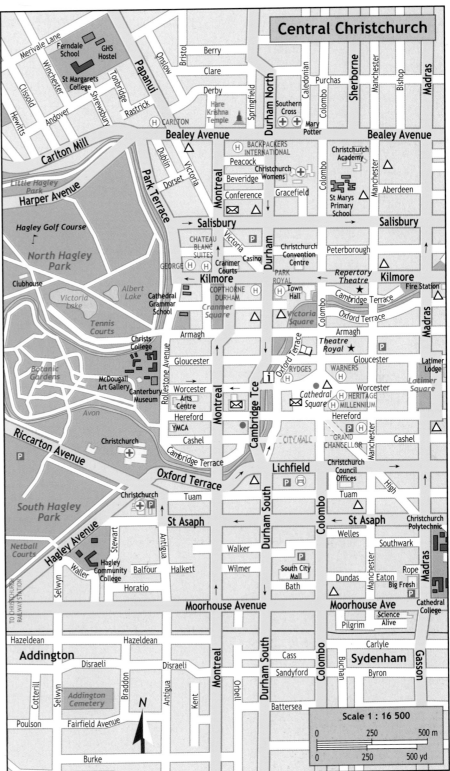

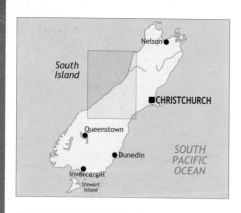

The West Coast

The West Coast of the South Island is a long, narrow region. Extending 600km from Karamea in the north to Cape Jackson in the south, 'the Coast' consists of a curving coastline backed by rainforest, snow-capped mountains, glaciers, alpine lakes and swift-flowing rivers. A highly scenic region with no cities, the Coast has five of New Zealand's thirteen national parks and in the far south is one of three UNESCO World Heritage Sites. The region's small towns are rich in history, as the Coast was the location for one of New Zealand's greatest gold rushes during the 1860s, when dozens of mining towns sprang up overnight.

MAIN ATTRACTIONS

- The unique formations of **Punakaiki's 'Pancake Rocks'**.
- Exploring the limestone landforms of the **Oparara Basin**.
- The pounamu (jade) carvings in **Hokitika's art galleries** and **craft shops** — modern examples of the ancient Maori craft of carving greenstone.

- The annual **Wild Food Festival** in Hokitika is a must for the strong of stomach.
- **Forest** and **beach walks**.
- Walking around **Kaniere Reserve**, a botanist's paradise.
- The bush surrounding **Lake Kaniere**, 17km from Hokitika, offers more than 50 specimens of ferns.

- Visiting the **fur seal colony** at Tauranga Bay.
- The magnificent **Franz Josef** and **Fox glaciers**.
- Experiencing spectacular **sunsets** over crashing surf on the beaches of the West Coast.
- The **lagoon** at Okarito, home of the **white heron**.

Right: *The spectacular formations of 'Pancake Rocks' at Punakaiki, Paparoa National Park, North Westland.*

ACCOMMODATION

Punakaiki Rocks Hotel & Villas, SH6, Punakaiki, tel: (03) 731 1168, fax: (03) 731 1163, e-mail: info@punakaiki-resort.co.nz website: www.punakaiki-resort.co.nz Beachfront location within Paparoa National Park.

Rimu Lodge, 33 Seddon Terrace Road, Rimu, Hokitika, tel: (03) 755 5255, fax: (03) 755 5237, e-mail: rimulodge@xtra.co.nz website: www.rimulodge.co.nz Luxury lodge, overlooking native forest.

Beachfront Hotel Hokitika, 111 Revell Street, Hokitika, tel: (03) 755 8344, freephone: 0800 400 344, fax: (03) 755 8258, e-mail: reservations@ beachfronthotel.co.nz website: www.beachfronthotel.co.nz Rooms and restaurant overlooking the Tasman Sea.

Formerly the Blackball Hilton, 26 Hart Street, Blackball, tel: (03) 732 4705, fax: (03) 732 4708, freephone: 0800 425 2252, e-mail: bbhilton@xtra.co.nz website: www.blackballhilton.co.nz A West Coast institution where visitors can meet the locals.

The West Coast

Scale 1 : 900 000

0   10   20 km
0   5   10 miles

2000 m+
1000–2000 m
500–1000 m
200–500 m
100–200 m
0–100 m

N

Tasman Sea

Karamea Bight

Westport
Cape Foulwind
Seal Colony ★ 67A
Cape Foulwind
Sergeants Hill
67
Tauranga Bay
Te Kuha
Nine Mile Beach
6
Charleston
Tiromoana
Kaipakati Point
Paparoa National Park
Maimai
PAPAROA RANGE
Hukarere
Dolomite Point Punakaiki
Pancake Rocks and Blowholes ★
Craigleburn
Barrytown
6
Greigs
Atarau
7
Nobles
Motukiekie Rocks
Roa
Rapahoe
Ngahere
Runanga
Kamaka
Dobson
Greymouth
Kokiri
Te Kinga
Lake Hochstetter
Lake Ahaura
Paroa
Gladstone
Mining Town Replica (Shantytown) ★
Bell Hill
Camerons
Greenstone
Te Kinga
Lake Poerua
Kumara Junction
Rotomanu
Awatuna
Taramakau
Poerua
Kaihinu
Goldsborough
Lake Brunner
Hokitika
Woodstock
Turiwhate
Wainihinihi
Jacksons
73
Mananui
Aickens
Ruatapu
Kowhitirangi
Lake Kaniere
Otira
Lookout
(Otira Viaduct) ★
Arthur's Pass National Park
Ross
Kaniere Reserve
Styx
Mt Rolleston
▲ 2271 m
Historic Gold Town ★
Hokitika
Arthur's Pass
Kakapotahi
Fergusons
Mt Findlay
▲ 1806 m
73
Pukekura
Waitaha
Bealey
Wanganui Bluff
Lake Ianthe
Mt Beaumont
▲ 2141 m
Craigieburn Forest Park
Saltwater Lagoon
Herepo
Poerua
Moa
Castle Hill
Kotuku (White Heron) Sanctuary ★
Harihari
RAGGED RANGE
Lake Coleridge
Rotokino
Okarito Lagoon
WILBERG RANGE
Blair Peak
▲ 2495 m
Rakaia
Okarito
Te Taho
The Forks
Blanchards Bluff
Whataroa
Westland/ Tai Poutini National Park
Lake Coleridge
SOUTHERN ALPS
Ashburton
Tatare
Franz Josef
CLOUDY PEAK
MT HUTT RANGE
Gillespies Point
Mt Alex
▲ 2271 m
The Point
Otorokua Point
Gillespies Beach
6
Lookout Point ★
Clyde
Mount Hutt
Fox Glacier
Cook
Erewhon
Emily Hill
▲ 964 m
Karangarua
Mt Tasman
▲ 3497 m
Aoraki/ Mt Cook National Park
SIBBALD RANGE
TWO THUMB RANGE
Lake Heron
72
Bruce Bay
Westland/ Tai Poutini National Park
Aoraki/
Mt Cook
▲ 3754 m
Lake Clearwater
Hakatere
Methven
Titiraha Head
Jacobs River
Copland
Mesopotamia
Mount Possession
Mt Somers
Staveley
CAPE JACKSON
Mahitahi
SOUTHERN ALPS
GAMMACK RANGE
HALL RANGE
Lilybank Station
FOUR PEAKS RANGE
Cavendish
Anama
Valetta
6
Lake Moeraki
Lake Paringa
STRACHAN RANGE
BANNOCK BRAE RANGE
Mount Cook Village
Hooker Glacier Lake Walk ★
Cass
Gray
Forest
Mt Peel
▲
Mayfield
77
Hackthorne
Moeraki
Otoko
Mt Hooker
▲ 2652 m
NEUMANN RANGE
BEN OHAU RANGE
80
Lake Tekapo
Lake Alexandrina
Clayton
Blandswood
72
Lagmhor
Law Peak
▲ 1981 m
Clarke
Wills
Tekapo Military Camp
Lake Tekapo
Lake Opuha
Ashwick Flat
Maronan
Carew
6
Wuzel
Lake Pukaki
Church of the Good Shepherd ★
Four Peaks
Te Moana
Woodbury
Arundel
Winslow
The Deuce
▲ 1577 m
Haast Pass
Burkes Pass
Rangitata
Geraldine
Hinds
Eiffelton
Ealing
1

Southern Alps and Lakes District

The South Island's Alps and lakes make up New Zealand's most imposing geographic region. The saw-toothed Alps include New Zealand's highest peak, Aoraki/Mount Cook (3754m), and neighbouring Mount Tasman (3497m). The Alps were shaped by glaciation during the Ice Age when moving glaciers filled the alpine valleys and carved them into U-shapes. When the climate became warmer, moraine was deposited in the valleys, blocking them, so that long deep lakes filled behind these deposits. Glacier-fed, shingle-bedded rivers pour from the Alps, their courses 'braided' into many channels, feeding the lakes and building up alluvial plains from the silt they carry.

Above: There is an array of adventure tourist activities available in the Queenstown region. You can participate in jet-boating, bungy jumping, hang-gliding, horse trekking, mountain biking, luge riding, heli-skiing, parasailing, parapenting, sky-diving, rafting, kayaking, river surfing, four-wheel-drive safaris, flying fox riding, hot-air ballooning and jet-skiing.

ACCOMMODATION

Heritage Hotel, 91 Fernhill Road, Queenstown, tel: (03) 442 4988, fax: (03) 442 4989, e-mail: reszqn@heritagehotels.co.nz website: www.heritagehotels.co.nz
Eichardt's Private Hotel, Marine Parade, Queenstown, tel: (03) 441 0450, fax: (03) 441 0440, email: enquiries@eichardtshotel.co.nz website: www.eichardtshotel.co.nz
Whare Kea Lodge and Chalet, Mount Aspiring Road, Wanaka, tel: (03) 443 1400, fax: (03) 443 9200, e-mail: admin@wharekealodge.com website: www.wharekealodge.com
Cardrona Hotel, Crown Range Road, RD1, Wanaka, tel: (03) 443 8153, fax (03) 443 8163, e-mail: info@ cardronahotel.co.nz website: www.cardronahotel.co.nz

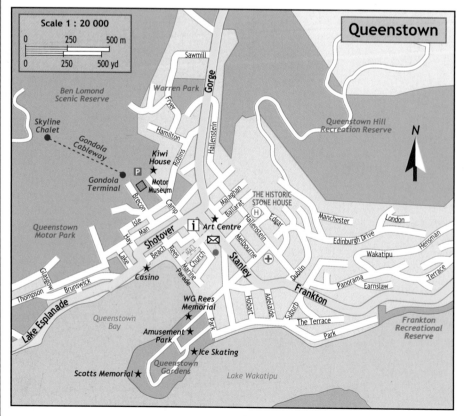

MAIN ATTRACTIONS

- **Skiing** on one of the region's skifields, such as Coronet Peak, the Remarkables, Cardrona or Treble Cone.
- A **jet boat ride** up one of the region's braided rivers.
- A **four-wheel-drive 'safari'** to Skippers Canyon.
- A **wine tour** of the Central Otago vineyards.
- A day in the pretty, **historic settlement** of Arrowtown.
- A trip on the **TSS** *Earnslaw*, on Lake Wakatipu.
- Watching the **sun set** over Lake Wakatipu from the lake's shore.
- **Hiking** up to Ben Lomond, above Queenstown, and savouring the **alpine views**.
- A **scenic flight** over the Alps and the Tasman Glacier.
- A three-day **hike** along the Routeburn Track.

Southern Alps and Lakes District

Scale 1 : 900 000

0   10   20 km
0   5   10 miles

2000 m+
1000–2000 m
500–1000 m
200–500 m
100–200 m
0–100 m

N

Mt Tasman
3497 m   Aoraki/
Mt Cook
3754 m

Westland/
Tai Poutini
National Park

Copland

Hooker Glacier

SOUTHERN ALPS

Jacobs River

Bruce Bay

Heretaniwha Point

Mahitahi

Makawhio

Blizzard Peak
2408 m   Mt Sefton
3157 m   ★ Hooker Glacier
Lake Walk

Mount Cook
Village

Mt Spence
2438 m

BANNOCK BRAE RANGE

Tititira Head

Piakatu Point

Abbey Rocks

Lake Paringa

6

STRACHAN RANGE

Mahitahi

Mt Humphries
2446 m

Mt Brown
2179 m ▲

80

Tasman

Knights Point

Lake Moeraki

Lake Paringa

Lake Moeraki

Paringa

Otoko

Clarke

NEUMANN RANGE

BEN OHAU RANGE

Dobson

Power Knob
1509 m

Paringa

Moeraki

Landsborough

Hopkins

Lake Pukaki

Haast Beach

Haast

Okuru

Bain Hill
115 m

Lake Douglas

Haast

Thomas

MATAKETAKE RANGE

6

Birch Knob
1020 m

Wills

Harris

Maitland

80

Mt Cook
Lookout
★

Pukaki

Jackson Bay

Jackson Head

Neils Beach

Waiatoto

Arawhata

Arawhata

HAAST RANGE

Turnbull

Okuru

Waiatoto

Ngatau

Souter Peak
1996 m

Mt Victor
1935 m

Burke

Mt Burke
1783 m

The Deuce
1577 m

Makarora

Burke

Mt Huxley
2499 m

Rabbiters Peak
2286 m

Ahuriri

The Pyramid
851 m

Twizel

Misty Peak
1897 m

Mt Aspiring
National Park

Siberia

Mt Achilles
1875 m

Mt Turner
2149 m

Mt Aeolus
2301 m

Wilkin

Makarora

Makarora

YOUNG RANGE

Waterfall

Hunter

BARRIER RANGE

Mt Rigel
2096 m

Lake Ohau
Lodge

Lake Ohau

Ohau

Clearburn

Lake Benmore

8

BENMORE RANGE

Fastness Peak

Mt Aspiring
2383 m

3033 m

Albert Burn

Big Hopwood Burn

2027 m
Terrace Peak

Boundary

Dingle Burn

2042 m

Clay Cliffs Walk

Ahuriri

Omarama

Swan Lagoon

The White
1765 m

Lake Wanaka

Lake Hawea

Dingle Peak
1833 m

Mt Prospect
1768 m

Dromedary Hill
1661 m

83

Otematata

Glengyle Peak
2377 m

Estuary Burn

Minaret Burn

2203 m

Twin Peaks
1653 m

Triple Peak

Mt Aspiring
★
Rob Roy Track

Mt Repulse
2203 m

Treble Cone
Skifield ★

1024 m

Smiths

Timaru

Dip

8

★ Lindis
Pass

ST BATHANS RANGE

HAWKDUN RANGE

Clear

Clear

Lake Hawea

Gladstone

Clutha

Camp

Rocks

1516 m

HARRIS MOUNTAINS

End Peak
2100 m

Glendhu Bay

Polnoon

Maungawera

Hawea Flat

Albert Town

Wanaka

6   ★ Skyshow Centre

Falls Dam

Boundary

Mt Aurum
2245 m

1733 m

Skippers Canyon ★

Arrow

Shotover

Cardrona

Mt Barker

8A

Lindis Valley

DUNSTAN MOUNTAINS

Dunstan

St Bathans

Mt Ida
1692 m

Middle Peak
1840 m

Luggate

8

Cluden

Cambrians

85

Cardrona
Skifield

Cardrona

Luggate

PISA RANGE

Queensberry

6

Tarras

Lindis

Wainui

Ardgour

Lauder

Drybread

Oturehua

Idaburn

Idaburn

Mt Gilbert
1783 m

Coronet Peak
▲ 1651 m

Coronet Skifield

Arrowtown

Wharehuanui

Crown Terrace

Park Burn

Low Burn

Mt Pisa

Mt Allen
1492 m

Bendigo

Crippletown

8

Lowburn

Lake Dunstan

Matakanui

Becks

Ida Valley

Wedderburn

Naseby

Ben Lomond

Skyline Gondola

Queenstown

Fernhill

Kelvin Heights

Remarkables Skifield

Mt Salmond
1640 m

Lake Wakatipu

Lower Shotover

Arrow Junction

Gibbston

6

Kawarau Bridge ★

Riponvale

Bannockburn

Cromwell

Dunstan
1667 m

Chatto

85

Omakau

Ophir

Ida Burn

Lauder

Ranfurly

Frankton

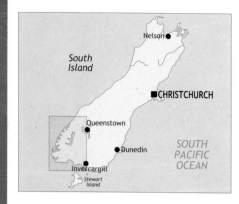

Fiordland

This remote, rugged region, which occupies the southwestern corner of the South Island, is named for the fourteen fiords which indent its coastline. The fiords were created by glaciers during the last Ice Age. When the Ice Age ended about 12,000 years ago, the sea flooded the sheer-sided valleys the glaciers had carved out, creating a series of deep-water 'sounds' or fiords. Fiordland is New Zealand's largest national park and has been designated a World Heritage Area. The region has immense geographic grandeur: deep fiords, towering mountains, waterfalls, 'hanging' valleys, glacial lakes and virgin beech forests.

Left: A cruise ship on the deep waters of Milford Sound. Mitre Peak, at 1692m, dominates the skyline above Milford Sound.
Opposite: Architectural highlights of Dunedin include its splendidly restored Victorian railway station.

ACCOMMODATION

Fiordland Lodge, 472 Te Anau Milford Highway, Te Anau, tel: (03) 249 7832, fax: (03) 249 7449, e-mail: info@fiordlandlodge.co.nz website: www.fiordlandlodge.co.nz Great views over Lake Te Anau and Fiordland National Park.

Campbell Autolodge, 42 Lakefront Drive, Te Anau, tel: (03) 249 7546, fax: (03) 249 7814, e-mail: reservations@cal.co.nz website: www.cal.co.nz Lake and mountain views.

Te Anau Lake View Holiday Park, 1 Te Anau Highway, Manapouri, Te Anau, freephone: 0800 4 Te Anau, tel: (03) 249 7457, fax: (03) 249 7536, e-mail: res@teanau.info website: www.fiordland.org.nz Lakeside, elevated location gives great views.

Fiordland Hotel & Motel Resort, corner Barnaby Place and Luxmore Drive, Te Anau, tel: (03) 249 7511, fax: (03) 249 8944, website: www.FiordlandHotel.co.nz Garden setting with views.

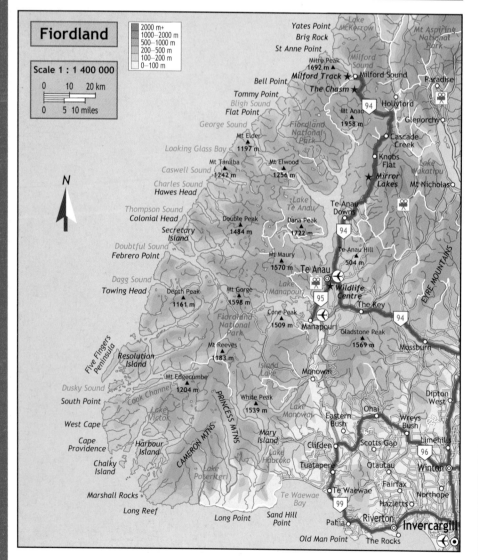

MAIN ATTRACTIONS

- The **four-day Milford Track**, from the head of Lake Te Anau to Milford Sound.
- A **cruise on Milford Sound**, an enclosed, misty world bordered by sheer rock walls.
- A **cruise on Lake Manapouri** and **Doubtful Sound**.
- A **helicopter flight** over Lake Te Anau and Milford Sound.

Central Dunedin

Dunedin was founded by Scottish immigrants in 1848, and named after the ancient Gaelic name for Edinburgh. In 1861 gold was discovered in Dunedin's hinterland, leading to an influx of fortune-seekers from all over the world descending on the region. For the next thirty years Dunedin was New Zealand's commercial capital and its largest city. Although it has long lost this status, Dunedin is noted as a major centre of tertiary education. Otago University has 19,000 students, many coming to Dunedin from other parts of New Zealand to live and study. The city's colonial heritage is evident in its many Victorian stone buildings and cultural centres, such as the Hocken Library, First Church of Otago, Saint Paul's Anglican Cathedral and the city's restored Railway Station. Dunedin's main retailing streets converge onto the central Octagon, which is overlooked by a statue of the renowned Scottish poet, Robbie Burns.

MAIN ATTRACTIONS

- **Olveston**, one of New Zealand's finest **historic homes**.
- The grand Victorian architecture of **Dunedin Railway Station** (1906).
- **Dunedin Public Art Gallery** houses famous European and New Zealand art collections.
- Dunedin's **Botanic Gardens** offer impressive plant collections.
- The **Otago Settlers Museum** tells the story of Dunedin's settlement and colonisation.

ACCOMMODATION

Corstorphine House, Milburn Street, Dunedin, tel: (03) 487 1000, fax: (03) 467 6672, e-mail: info@corstorphine.co.nz website: www.corstorphine.co.nz Luxurious facilities amid a large estate.
Glenfield House, 3 Peel Street, Mornington, Dunedin, tel: (03) 453 5923, e-mail: glenfieldhouse@xtra.co.nz website: www.glenfieldhouse.co.nz Victorian boutique accommodation.
Albatross Inn, 770 George Street, Dunedin, tel: (03) 477 2727, fax: (03) 477 2108, e-mail: info@albatross.inn.co.nz website: www.albatross.inn.co.nz Edwardian elegance close to the city centre.
For **further information** on accommodation and dining establishments in Dunedin, log on to the website: www.cityofdunedin.com

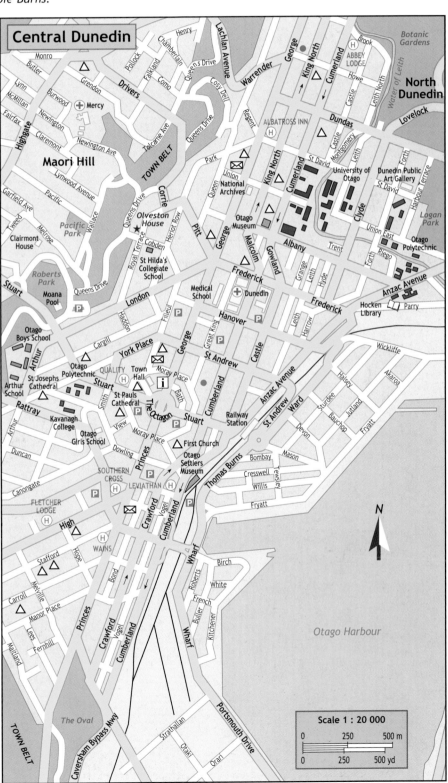

Scale 1 : 20 000

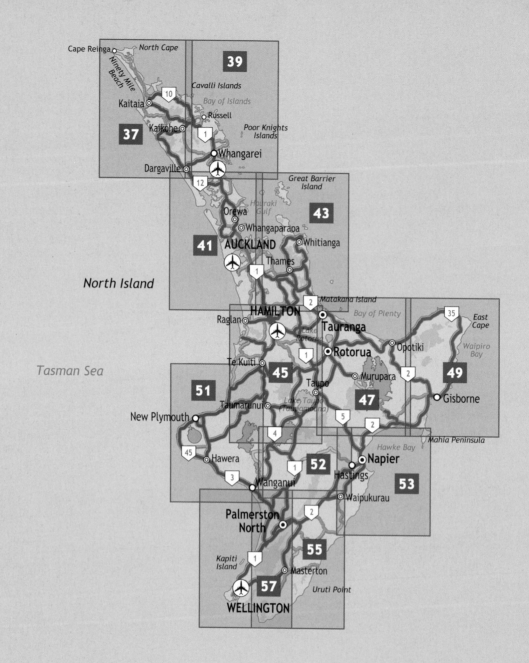

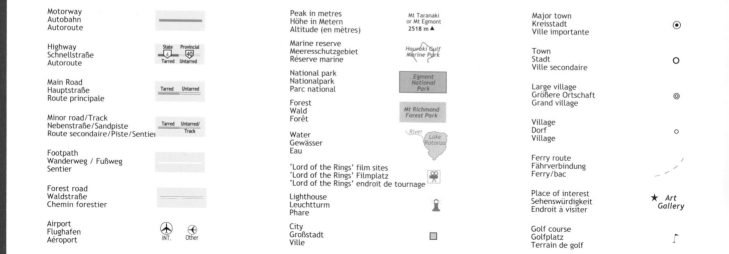

Motorway Autobahn Autoroute		Peak in metres Höhe in Metern Altitude (en mètres)	Mt Taranaki or Mt Egmont 2518 m ▲	Major town Kreisstadt Ville importante ◉
Highway Schnellstraße Autoroute	State	Provincial 40 Tarred Untarred	Marine reserve Meeresschutzgebiet Réserve marine	Hauraki Gulf Marine Park	Town Stadt Ville secondaire ○
Main Road Hauptstraße Route principale	Tarred Untarred	National park Nationalpark Parc national	Egmont National Park	Large village Größere Ortschaft Grand village ◎
Minor road/Track Nebenstraße/Sandpiste Route secondaire/Piste/Sentier	Tarred Untarred/ Track	Forest Wald Forêt	Mt Richmond Forest Park	Village Dorf Village ○
Footpath Wanderweg / Fußweg Sentier		Water Gewässer Eau	River Lake Rotorua	Ferry route Fährverbindung Ferry/bac
Forest road Waldstraße Chemin forestier		'Lord of the Rings' film sites 'Lord of the Rings' Filmplatz 'Lord of the Rings' endroit de tournage	🎥	Place of interest Sehenswürdigkeit Endroit à visiter ★ Art Gallery
Airport Flughafen Aéroport	✈ ✈ INT. Other	Lighthouse Leuchtturm Phare		Golf course Golfplatz Terrain de golf
		City Großstadt Ville	▢	

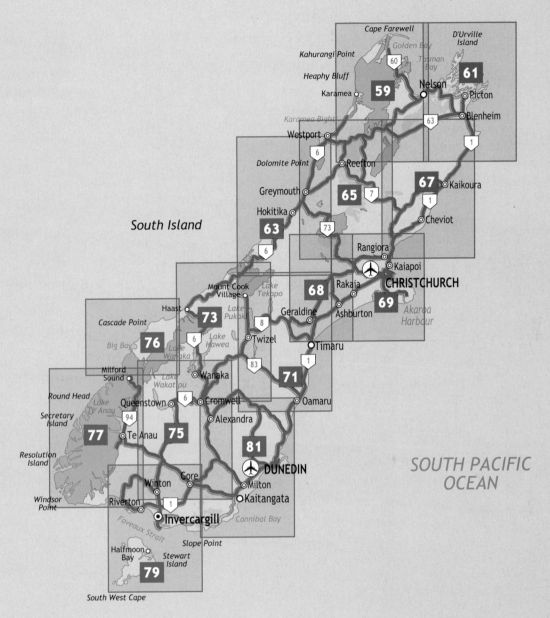

South Island

Cape Farewell
D'Urville Island
Kahurangi Point
Golden Bay
Heaphy Bluff
Tasman Bay
Karamea
59
Nelson
61
Picton
Karamea Bight
Blenheim
Westport
63
6
Dolomite Point
Reefton
65 7
67
Kaikoura
1
Greymouth
Cheviot
Hokitika
63
73
6
Rangiora
Mount Cook Village
Lake Tekapo
68
Kaiapoi
CHRISTCHURCH
Haast
73
Lake Pukaki
Rakaia
69
Cascade Point
76
Geraldine
Ashburton
Akaroa Harbour
Big Bay
6
Lake Hawea
8
Twizel
71
Mitford Sound
Lake Wanaka
83
Timaru
1
Round Head
Wanaka
Queenstown
6
Cromwell
Oamaru
Lake Te Anau
94
Secretary Island
Alexandra
77
Te Anau
75
81
Resolution Island
Lake Wakatipu
DUNEDIN
Windsor Point
Winton
Gore
Milton
Riverton
1
Kaitangata
Invercargill
Foveaux Strait
Cannibal Bay
Slope Point
Halfmoon Bay
Stewart Island
79
South West Cape

SOUTH PACIFIC OCEAN

N

National route	
Main route	
Main route untarred	
Provincial boundary	
Route Number	6
Airport	✈
City, town & village	☐ ◉ ○ ◎
Main map section page layout	**47**

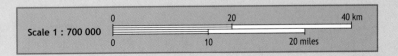

Scale 1 : 700 000

| 0 | 20 | 40 km |
| 0 | 10 | 20 miles |

Northland

Northland is a region which is easy to explore by car. Good roads follow both the west and east coasts, and crossing from one coast to the other provides an interesting contrast in landscapes and coastlines. The Twin Coast Discovery Highway is a touring route that provides a great round trip through Northland. Central to the west coast is the Hokianga Harbour, where giant golden sand dunes are found at the northern harbour entrance and there is a charming town, Rawene. The east coast has many beautiful, sheltered beaches such as Matapouri, Matauri Bay, Taipa Bay, Coopers Beach, Matai Bay and Houhora.

ACCOMMODATION

Pacific Rendezvous, Tutukaka, tel: (09) 434 3847, fax: (09) 434 3919, freephone: 0800 999 800, e-mail: pacific@igrin.co.nz website: www.pacificrendezvous.co.nz A resort atop a headland.
Eagles Nest, 60 Tapeka Road, Russell, Bay of Islands, tel: (09) 403 8333, fax: (09) 403 8880, e-mail: manager@ eaglesnest.co.nz website: www.eagles nest.co.nz A world-class resort with panoramic views of the Bay of Islands.
Mangonui Hotel, 8 Waterfront Road, Mangonui, tel: (09) 406 0003, fax: (09) 406 0015, e-mail: mangonuihotel@xtra. co.nz A traditional Kiwi hotel.
Cavalli Beach House, Mahinepua Road, RDI Kaeo, tel: (09) 405 1049, fax: (09) 405 1043, e-mail: carrie@cavallibeachhouse.com website: www.cavallibeachhouse.com

Above: *These giant kauri trees are to be found in the Waipoua Kauri Forest, Trounson Kauri Forest in western Northland, and in parts of Coromandel.*
Left: *The golden sand dunes on Hokianga Harbour's North Head are a striking landmark.*

TRAVEL TIPS

If travelling by road, the **'Twin Coast Discovery Highway'** is a great way to see the best of Northland. The route is well signposted and takes the visitor along both the west and east coasts of the region, taking in such attractions as the Waipoua Forest, the Hokianga Harbour, Doubtless Bay and the Bay of Islands along the way. Stopovers can be made at the coastal settlements of Opononi, Ahipara, Mangonui and Russell. A trip on the car ferry across the Hokianga Harbour from Rawene township saves travel time when driving north to Kaitaia and Ninety Mile Beach.

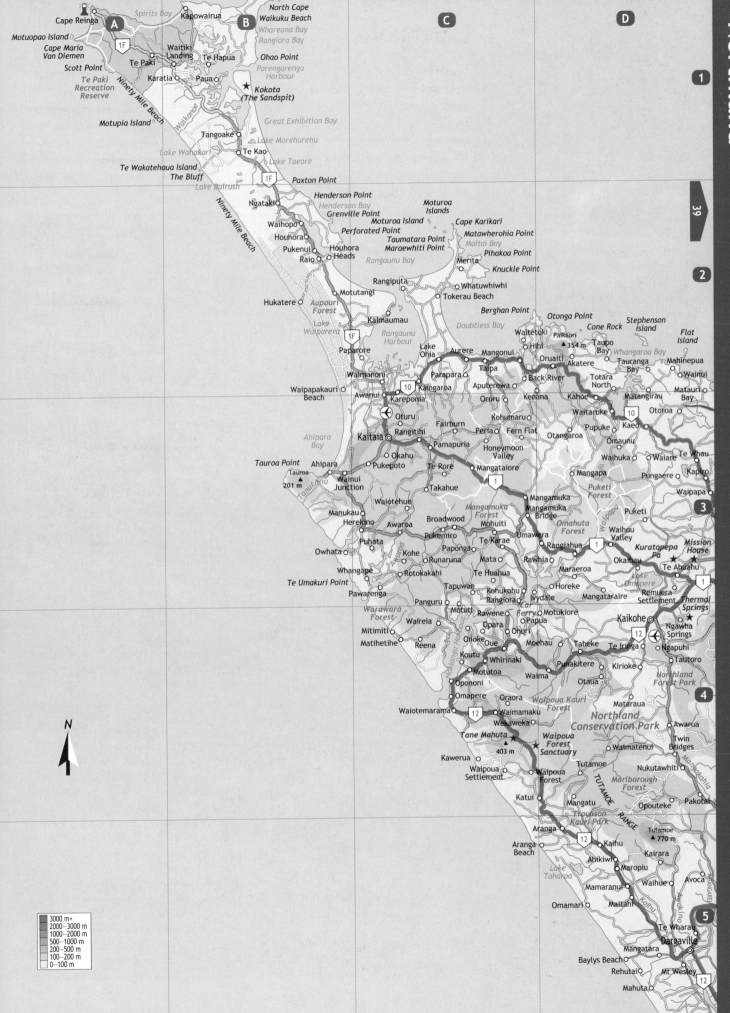

A   B   C   D

1

39

2

3

4

5

Cape Reinga
Motuopao Island
Cape Maria Van Diemen
Scott Point
Te Paki Recreation Reserve
Spirits Bay
Kapowairua
Waitiki Landing
Te Paki
Te Hapua
Karatia
Paua
North Cape
Waikuku Beach
Whareana Bay
Rangiora Bay
Ohao Point
Parengarenga Harbour
Kokota (The Sandspit)
Motupia Island
Great Exhibition Bay
Tangoake
Lake Morehurehu
Lake Wahakari
Te Kao
Lake Teaore
Te Wakatehaua Island
The Bluff
Lake Bulrush
Paxton Point
Ngataki
Henderson Point
Henderson Bay
Grenville Point
Waihopo
Moturoa Islands
Houhora
Perforated Point
Moturoa Island
Pukenui
Houhora Heads
Taumatara Point
Maraewhiti Point
Cape Karikari
Matawherohia Point
Maitai Bay
Pihakoa Point
Raio
Rangaunu Bay
Merita
Knuckle Point
Motutangi
Rangiputa
Whatuwhiwhi
Hukatere
Aupouri Forest
Kaimaumau
Tokerau Beach
Berghan Point
Lake Waiparera
Otonga Point
Cone Rock
Stephenson Island
Flat Island
Paparore
Rangaunu Harbour
Lake Ohia
Aurere
Waitetoki
Hihi
Pakauri
354 m
Taupo Bay
Whangaroa Bay
Mahinepua
Wainui
Waipapakauri Beach
Waimanoni
Parapara
Taipa
Mangonui
Oruaiti
Akatere
Tauranga Bay
Matauri Bay
Awanui
Kaingaroa
Aputerewa
Back River
Totara North
Matangirau
Oturu
Kareponia
Oruru
Kenana
Kahoe
Waitaruke
Otoroa
Kaitaia
Rangitihi
Fairburn
Kohumaru
Perla
Fern Flat
Otangaroa
Pupuke
Kaeo
Okahu
Pamapuria
Honeymoon Valley
Mangapa
Waihuka
Waiare
Te Whau
Ahipara
Pukepoto
Te Rore
Mangataiore
Puketi Forest
Pungaere
Kapiro
Tauroa Point
Tauroa
201 m
Ahipara Bay
Wainui Junction
Takahue
Puketi
Waipapa
Waiotehue
Mangamuka Forest
Mangamuka
Mangamuka Bridge
Omahuta Forest
Waihou Valley
Manukau
Herekino
Awaroa
Broadwood
Mohuiti
Umawera
Rangiahua
Kuratopepa Pa
Mission House
Puhata
Pukemiro
Te Karae
Rawhia
Maraeroa
Okaihau
Te Ahuahu
Owhata
Kohe
Paponga
Mata
Te Huahua
Maraeroa
Horeke
Lake Omapere
Remuera Settlement
Runaruna
Whangape
Rotokakahi
Tapuwae
Kohukohu
Rangiora
Ivydale
Mangataraire
Thermal Springs
Te Umakuri Point
Panguru
Motuti
Rawene
Papua
Motukiore
Kaikohe
Pawarenga
Waireia
Car Ferry
Ngawha Springs
Warawara Forest
Mitimiti
Opara
Onoke
Ohuri
Moehau
Taheke
Te Iringa
Ngapuhi
Matihetihe
Reena
Oue
Whirinaki
Punakitere
Kirioke
Tautoro
Koutu
Waima
Otaua
Northland Forest Park
Motutoa
Opononi
Omapere
Oraora
Waimamaku
Mataraua
Awarua
Waiotemarama
Wekaweka
Waipoua Kauri Forest
Northland Conservation Park
Twin Bridges
Tane Mahuta
403 m
Waipoua Forest Sanctuary
Waimatenui
Nukutawhiti
Kawerua
Waipoua Settlement
Tutamoe
Marlborough Forest
Mangokahia
Katui
Mangatu
Tutamoe Range
Opouteke
Pakotai
Aranga
770 m
Trounson Kauri Park
Aranga Beach
Kaihu
Kairara
Ahikiwi
Maropiu
Lake Taharoa
Mamaranui
Waihue
Avoca
Omamari
Maitahi
Kaihu
Wairoa
Te Wharau
Whangarei
Dargaville
Baylys Beach
Mangatara
Rehutai
Mahuta
Mt Wesley

N

3000 m+
2000–3000 m
1000–2000 m
500–1000 m
200–500 m
100–200 m
0–100 m

Bay of Islands and Whangarei

The city of Whangarei, two hours by car from Auckland, makes a good base for exploring Northland. The most appealing part of the city is the Town Basin, a marina, retail and restaurant complex within walking distance of the central business district. New Zealand's only oil refinery is located at nearby Marsden Point, and the city also specializes in marine industries. There is a series of superb beaches, at Ngunguru, Tutukaka and Matapouri, to the northeast of Whangarei, all of which have a wide range of visitor accommodation. This subtropical region also has a growing reputation for its fine food and wines.

MAIN ATTRACTIONS

- Diving the **wreck** of the *Rainbow Warrior*, in the Cavalli Islands.
- Visiting the **Treaty House** and **Maori meeting house** at Waitangi.
- Dining at sunset on the **waterfront** at Russell.
- The **monument and views** from Flagstaff Hill, above Russell.
- Taking the **car ferry** from Opua across the bay.
- The **Frederick Hundertwasser-designed public toilets**, Kawakawa.
- **Surfing** at Sandy Bay, near Matapouri.
- The **drive** out to the beach at Bream Head, southeast of Whangarei.
- Strolling and **dining** at the Town Basin, Whangarei, which has a variety of shops, museums, cafés and restaurants.

Above: *A beautiful sight — the sun setting in splendour at the marina, Whangarei. The marina is part of Whangarei's Town Basin, which is home to an interesting variety of shops and restaurants.*

Right: *Anchorage and beach, Moturua Island, Bay of Islands. One of New Zealand's premier visitor destinations, the Bay of Islands provides a superb cruising environment for pleasure craft of all kinds. The many sheltered bays also offer excellent opportunities for swimming and fishing.*

TRAVEL TIPS

There are three **airports** in Northland: one at Whangarei, one at Kerikeri (Bay of Islands) and one at Kaitaia. Flight time from Auckland to Whangarei is 35 minutes and to Kerikeri 45 minutes. Driving time from Auckland to Paihia, in the Bay of Islands, is four hours and 15 minutes.
Website: www.northlandnz.com

A   B   C   D

1

2

3

4

5

37

41

3000 m+
2000–3000 m
1000–2000 m
500–1000 m
200–500 m
100–200 m
0–100 m

N

Wreck of "Rainbow Warrior"
★ Nukutaunga Island
Flat Island
Motukawanui Island
Cavalli Islands
Matauri Bay
Motukawaiti Island
Motuiwi Island
Te Pene
Takou Bay
Takou Bay
Taronui Bay
Otaha
Rocky Point
Purerua Peninsula
Te Whau
Te Tii
Purerua
Cape Wiwiki
Bay of Islands Maritime and Historic Park
Kapiro
Howe Point
Cape Brett
Motukokako Island (Piercy Island)
Waipapa
Moturoa Island
Moturua Island
Bay of Islands
Waiwiri Island
Kerikeri
Net Rock
Kerikeri Inlet
★ Stone House
Rawhiti
Treaty House
★ Waitangi
10
Russell
Haruru
Paihia
Whangamumu Point
Te Waimate Mission ★ House
Puketona
Paroa Bay
Parekura Bay
Otao
Okiato
Taupiri Bay
Opua
Oromahoe
Waihaha
Tutaematai
Home Point
1
Whangae
Waikare
Whangaruru North
Pakaraka
Hupara
▲ 166 m
Whangaruru
Bland Bay
Kawakawa
Punaruku
Okaoko Rock
★ Thermal Springs
Moerewa
Oakura
Whangaruru Harbour
★ Ngawha Springs
Kawiti
Waiomio
Mokau
Motukehua Island
Pokapu
Helena Bay
Rimariki Island
Ruapekapeka
Poor Knights Islands Marine Reserve
Northland Forest Park
Taikirau
Tapuhi
Roimata Point
Tawhiti Rahi Island
Opahi
Towai
Akerama
Kaimamaku
Poor Knights Islands
Motatau
Hukerenui
Whananaki
Aorangi Island
Matawaia
Paiaka
Motutara Point
Marlow
Waiotu
Opuawhanga
High Peak Rocks
1
Whakapara
Sandys Bay
Sandy Bay
Sugarloaf Rock
Riponui
Otonga
Kaikou
Waro
Waipaipai
Tanekaha
Hikurangi
Kaiatea
Tutukaka
Pipiwai
Otakairangi
Ngunguru
Purua
Apotu
Kauri
Moengawahine
Matarau
Kamo
Glenbervie
Tahere
Horahora
Three Mile Bush
★ Whangarei Falls
Whareora
Ngunguru Bay
Pakotai
Parakao
Titoki
Roroti
Whangarei
Waiparera
Pataua North
Houto
Maungatapere
Waikaraka
Taiharuru
Wharekohe
Otaika
Onerahi
Parua Bay
Avoca
Whatitiri
Awarua Rock
Tangiteroria
Portland
Whangarei Harbour
McLeod Bay
14
Waiotama
Oakleigh
Reotahi Bay
Ocean Beach
Kirikopuni
Mangapai
Mata
Marsden Bay
Marsden Point
Tangihua
1
Busby Head
Marotere Islands
Tangowahine
Pukehuia
Tauroa
Taurarua
Springfield
Te Wharau
Pikiwahine
Waipu Caves
Ruakaka
Hen and Chicken Islands
Dargaville
Windy Hill
Waiotira
North River
Bream Bay
Turiwiri
Arapohue
Okahu
Waikiekie
Ruarangi
Taranga Island
12
Taipuha
Braigh
Waipu
AUCKLAND
Bream Tail
Hauraki Gulf Marine Park

Auckland and Surrounds

Auckland is New Zealand's largest industrial and commercial centre. The many employment opportunities which the city offers, along with its mild maritime climate and attractive coastlines, have attracted thousands of migrants from overseas countries and the rest of New Zealand in recent years. Most overseas visitors arriving by air come first to Auckland Airport, which is serviced by 20 international carriers, with direct flights from 31 cities. Auckland is the world's largest Polynesian city, with twenty percent of its population being Maori, Samoan, Tongan, Cook Island or Niuean.

MAIN ATTRACTIONS

- **Tiritiri Matangi Island**, off the Whangaparaoa Peninsula, a sanctuary for **endangered native birds**.
- **Wenderholm Regional Park**, just north of Waiwera bridge, for **swimming, picnicking, kayaking** and **bush walks**.
- **Hiking** through the **Waitakere Ranges**, west of Auckland.
- Soaking in the **thermal pools** at **Parakai**, near Helensville, and **Waiwera**, near Orewa.
- **Shopping** in the **Otara Market**, in south Auckland, on a Saturday morning.
- **Bird-watching** at **Miranda**, on the Firth of Thames (*see* map p. 43).
- The west-coast beaches of **Muriwai, Piha** and **Karekare**.

Right: *A takahe, an endangered native bird, roams free on Tiritiri Matangi Island, Hauraki Gulf. The island is now a predator-free habitat for many of New Zealand's native birds.*

USEFUL CONTACTS

Auckland i-SITE Visitor Centre, SkyCity, cnr Victoria & Federal Streets, tel: (09) 363 7182.
Auckland i-SITE Visitor Centre, Princes Wharf, cnr Quay & Hobson Streets, tel: (09) 307 0612.
Auckland i-SITE Visitor Centre, Air NZ Domestic Terminal, Auckland Airport, tel: (09) 256 8480.
Auckland i-SITE Visitor Centre, International Terminal, Auckland Airport, tel: (09) 275 6467.
Devonport i-SITE Visitor Centre, 3 Victoria Road, Devonport, tel: (09) 446 0677.
Takapuna i-SITE Visitor Centre, 49 Hurstmere Road, Takapuna, tel: (09) 486 8670.

ACCOMMODATION

Waiwera Infinity Thermal Spa Resort, 21 Main Road, Waiwera, tel: (09) 427 8800, fax: (09) 427 8816, e-mail: mail@waiwera.co.nz website: www.waiwera.co.nz Thermal pools and comfortable accommodation, 25 minutes north of the Harbour Bridge.
Parklane Motor Inn, cnr Lake Road and Rewiti Avenue, Takapuna, tel: (09) 486 1069, fax: (09) 486 2658, website: www.parklane.co.nz On the North Shore, handy to Takapuna beach and motorway connections.

Barrycourt Suites Hotel & Conference Centre, 10-20 Gladstone Road, Parnell, Auckland, tel: (09) 303 3789, fax: (09) 377 3309, e-mail: barrycourt@xtra.co.nz website: www.barrycourt.co.nz A wide range of accommodation types is available here; close to Parnell Road shops and the Domain.
Palm Beach Lodge, 23 Tiri View Road, Waiheke Island, tel/fax: (09) 372 7763, e-mail: palmbeachlodge@xtra.co.nz website: www.waiheke.co.nz/palmbch.htm This establishment offers views of Waiheke's loveliest beach.

A

Koremoa
Tikinui
Ruawai
Raupo
Tokatoka
DARGAVILLE

Taingaehe
Te Kowhai
Burgess
Island
Matakohe
Pahi
Kauri and
Pioneer
Museum
B
12
Hukatere
Whakapirau

Rototuna
Arapaoa
Tanoa
Batley
Kaipara
Harbour
Matihe
Point

Pouto
Lake
Kanono
Lake
Humuhumu

Lake
Mokeno

North Head
Kaipara
Head
South Head
South Head

Rangitira
Beach
Waioneke
Lake
Ototoa
Orongo
Point
Glorit

Shelly
Beach
Oyster
Point
Lake
Kereta
179 m
Thermal
Pools
16
Parakai
Te Pua
Helensville

Lake
Ngakaru

Wharepapa
Woodhill
Waimauku
166 m
Huapai
Vineyards
Taupaki
16

Muriwai Beach
Gannet Colony
Waitakere

Te Henga
Swanson
Waitakere Ranges
Regional Park

Anawhata
Piha
Waiatarua

Karekare
Huia
Laingholm

Whatipu
Orua
Bay
Grahams
Beach

Awhitu
Central
Awhitu
Seagrove

Matakawau
Clarks
Beach
Waiau
Pa

Pollok
Te Toro
Glenbrook
Beach

Kohekohe
Steam
Railway
Glenbrook

Waipipi
Waiuku
Pukeoware

Taurangaruru
Whiriwhiri
Aka Aka

Otaua
Te Kohanga

Tauranganui
Waiuku
Forest
Mairoa
Sands

Port
Waikato
Wairamarama

Ngatutura Point
Kapiapia Rock
Waikaretu

Otehe
(Crayfish Point)

Tokatoka
WHANGAREI
Tara
C
Mangawhai
39
D

Huarau
Maungaturoto
Hakaru

Marohemo
Kaiwaka
Te Arai Point
Te Arai Point
Little Barrier
Island
1

Topuni
Te Arai
Tomarata
Te Titoki Point

Oruawharo
Port Albert
Waiteitei
Pakiri
Goat Island
Goat Island Marine Reserve
Cape Rodney

Onerini
Wellsford
Whangaripo
Leigh

Wharehine
Hoteo
North
Wayby
Valley
Whangateau
Ti Point
Omaha Bay

Tapora
Tauhoa
Waiwhiu
Matakana
Omaha
Takatu Point

Mangakura
Kaipara
Flats
Warkworth
Tawharanui

16
Kourawhera
Snells
Beach
Kawau
Bay
Kawau
Island

Parry Kauri Park
Woodcocks
Algies
Bay
Kawau Point

Komokoriki
Ahuroa
Pohuebue
Mahurangi
Motuora Island

Araparera
Puhoi
Mahurangi
West
Wenderholm
Regional Park

Makarau
Tahekeroa
Waiwera
Thermal Resort

Kanohi
Wainui
Silverdale
Orewa
Whangaparaoa
Bay
Tiritiri Matangi
Island

Kaukapakapa
Red
Beach
Hauraki Gulf

Loch
Norrie
Waitoki
Stillwater
Okura
Whangaparaoa
The Noises

Coatesville
Dairy
Flat
Redvale
Torbay
Motutapu
Island
Rakino
Island
43

Albany
Rangitoto
Island
Waiheke
Island
Palm
Beach

Riverhead
Kumeu
1
Takapuna
Oneroa
Ostend
Omiha

Whenuapai
18
Birkenhead
Browns
Island
Motuihe
Island
Tamaki
Strait

Ponsonby
Waitemata
Harbour
Devonport
AUCKLAND
Omana
Beach
3

Auckland
Zoo
Museum of
Transport and
Technology
Glen
Innes
Howick
Beachlands
Maraetai

Avondale
New Lynn
One Tree
Hill
East
Tamaki
Whitford
Brookby
Clevedon

20
Mangere
Papatoetoe
Manukau
Alfriston

Cornwallis
Manukau Harbour
Manurewa
1
Papakura
Hunua

Weymouth
Karaka
Drury

Te Hihi
22
Runciman

Kingseat
Ramarama
Ararimu
Paparata

Paerata
Bombay

Patumahoe
Puni
Pukekohe
Buckland

Tuakau
Pokeno
Whangarata

Pukekawa
Mercer

Onewhero
Meremere

Tauranganui
Orton
1

Glen
Murray
Opuatia
Churchill

Limestone
Downs
Naike

Woodleigh
Ruawaro
Pukekapia
5

Pepepe
Renown
Lake
Waahi

Rotowaro
Glen Afton
Te Akatea
Dunmore

N

3000 m+
2000–3000 m
1000–2000 m
500–1000 m
200–500 m
100–200 m
0–100 m

39

45

Hauraki Gulf and the Coromandel

Many Aucklanders own pleasure boats which they use for fishing, sailing or cruising on Manukau or Waitemata Harbour. Hence the name 'The City of Sails' is often applied to Auckland. The islands of the Hauraki Gulf lie close to the hearts of most Aucklanders, who can visit them in their own boats or by ferries which leave regularly from downtown Auckland. The Hauraki Gulf is a recreational area with a clean blue environment and many sheltered anchorages. From the Hauraki Gulf another landform is omnipresent on Auckland's eastern horizon — the rugged profile of the Coromandel Peninsula. Many Aucklanders have holiday houses there.

MAIN ATTRACTIONS

- Cruising the waters of the **Hauraki Gulf** and anchoring off one of its many picturesque islands.
- **Climbing** to the summit of the **extinct volcano, Rangitoto**, for magnificent views of Auckland.
- **Hiking** to **Stony Batter headland** on Waiheke Island to view the entire Hauraki Gulf, the Firth of Thames and the Coromandel Peninsula.
- **Climbing** to the summit of **Mount Hobson**, the highest point on **Great Barrier Island.**
- Sampling the **wines** and dining at the café of one of Waiheke Island's wineries.
- The **hike** across the northern extremity of the **Coromandel Peninsula**, from Port Charles to Port Jackson.
- Digging your own hot pool in the sand at low tide at **Hot Water Beach**, on the Coromandel Peninsula.
- Viewing the ancient square **kauri tree** on the Tapu to Coroglen Road.

Top right: Pleasure boats off Waiheke Island, Hauraki Gulf. A typical bay on Waiheke Island includes sheltered coves and sandy beaches.

TRAVEL TIPS

If you are **boating** on the Hauraki Gulf, listen to the marine weather forecasts, as **sea conditions** can change rapidly. When **driving** to the Coromandel from Auckland, travel at off-peak periods to avoid congestion during peak periods. The **ferries** which connect Auckland city with the islands of the Hauraki Gulf and the Coromandel leave from behind the **Ferry Building**, in Quay Street, in downtown Auckland, and the Viaduct Basin. Timetables are available in the Information Centre in front of the Ferry Building ticket office.

ACCOMMODATION

Miranda Holiday Park: 595 Front Miranda Road, Waitakaruru, tel/fax: (07) 867 3205, e-mail: office@mirandaholidaypark.co.nz website: www.mirandaholidaypark.co.nz This establishment consists of self-contained rural chalets alongside hot mineral pools.
Admirals Arms Hotel: 146 Wharf Road, Coromandel, tel/fax: (07) 866 8272, e-mail: nyden@paradise.net.nz A completely refurbished Victorian-era hotel.

Albert Cove: Waiheke Island, tel/fax: (09) 372 3523, e-mail: information@albertcove.com website: www.albertcove.com Luxury cottages set among trees and gardens at Putiki Bay, Waiheke Island.
Oasis Lodge: 50 Medlands Road, Tryphena, Great Barrier Island, tel: (09) 429 0021, fax: (09) 429 0034, e-mail: enquiries@barrieroasis.co.nz website: www.barrieroasis.net Casually elegant accommodation in a bush and vineyard setting.

USEFUL CONTACTS

Coromandel i-SITE Visitor Centre: 355 Kapanga Road, Coromandel, tel: (07) 866 8598, website: www.thecoromandel.com
Thames i-SITE Visitor Centre: 206 Pollen Street, Thames, tel: (07) 868 7284.
Whangamata i-SITE Visitor Centre: 16 Port Road, Whangamata, tel: (07) 865 8340.
Whitianga i-SITE Visitor Centre: 66 Albert Street, Whitianga, tel: (07) 866 5555.

A B C D

1
2
3
4
5

SOUTH
PACIFIC OCEAN

N

Katherine Bay
Maunganui Point
Hingaia Point
East Cape
Cradock Channel
Kaikoura Island
Kawa
Okiwi
Port Fitzroy
Mt Hobson
Whangaparapara
Broken Islands
Whangara Island
Okupu
Claris
Shag Point
Tryphena
Cape Barrier
Motairehe
Hautapu Point
Rakitu Island
Whakatautuna Point
Red Bluff
Awana Bay
Great Barrier Island

Colville Channel

Channel Island
Square Top Island
Cape Colville
Kaiiti Point
Port Jackson
Port Charles
Rauporoa Bay
Te Anaputa Point
Potiki Bay
375 m
Waiaro
Waikawau
Waikawau Bay
Haupapa Point
Arimawhai Point
Mercury Islands
Great Mercury Island
Double Island
Red Mercury Island
Korapuki Island

Hauraki Gulf Marine Park
Coromandel Forest Park
MOEHAU RANGE
Hauraki Gulf
Motukahaua Island
Motukawao Group
Little Bay
264 m
Colville
Kennedy Bay
Tuateawa
Anarake Point
Motuhua Point
Tokarahu Point
Opito
Ohinauiti Island
Ohinau Island

41

Horuhoru Rock
Thumb Point
Stony Batter
Waiheke Island
Onetangi
Omiha
Cowes
Orapiu
Tamaki Strait
Maraetai
Pakihi Island
Raukura Point
Orere Point
Ponui Island
Kawakawa Bay
Ness Valley
477 m
Matingarahi Point
Moturua Island
Motuoruhi Island
Whanganui Island
Tarahiki Island
Rotoroa Island
Coromandel Harbour
Deadmans Point
Kirita Bay
Papaaroha
Coromandel
Te Rerenga
Matarangi
Whangapoua
Kuaotunu
Motukoranga Island
COROMANDEL PENINSULA
Te Kouma
Whitianga
Mercury Bay
Mahurangi Island
25

Hunua
HUNUA RANGES
Whakatiwai
Kaiaua
Firth of Thames
Mahakirau
Kaimarama
Mill Creek
Coroglen
Te Mata Tapu
Waikawau
Kereta
Manaia
COROMANDEL RANGE
Tapu
Te Puru
Waiwawa
Kapowai
Paraku
Cooks Beach
Hahei
Castle Island
Hot Water Beach
Whenuakite
Te Ororoa Point
Hongiora Island
Ruamahuanui Island
The Aldermen Islands
Shoe Island
Ruamahuaiti Island
Tairua
Pauanui
Slipper Island
Penguin Island
Rabbit Island
25

Ruamahanga
Waiomu
Te Puru
Ngarimu Bay
Tararu 695 m
Whakatete Bay
Tararu
Coromandel Forest Park
Kauaeranga
Hikuai
Puketui
Ohui
Opoutere
Wharekawa Harbour
Onemana
Whitipirorua Point
Patuhamo Point

Happy Valley
Paparimu
Miranda
Miranda Hot Springs
Waitakaruru
Mangatangi
Mangatawhiri
Mangatangi
Maramarua
Kopuku
2
25
Orongo
Pipiroa
Kopu
Matatoki
Turua
Puriri
Wharekawa
Thames
COROMANDEL RANGE
Tairua
416 m
Whangamata
Parakiwai
Waiharakeke
Whangamata Harbour
Whenuakura Island
Wharepoa
Omahu
Hikutaia
Coromandel Forest Park
Pajakorahi
Whiritoa
Homunga Bay
Orokawa Bay
Mataora Bay
Mayor Island (Tuhua)
Tokimataa Point

Mangatawhiri
Mangatarata
Horahia
Ngatea
Kerepehi
Netherton
Komata North
Maratoto
Golden Cross
Waitekauri
Golden Valley
25
27
Okaeria
Torehape
Kaihere
Komata
Paeroa
Waikino
Waihi
Waihi Beach
Athenree
Pios Beach
Katikati Entrance
2

Whangamarino
Te Kauwhata
Waerenga
Taniwha
Rangiriri
Matahuru
Lake Waikare
Mangapiko Valley
Waiterimu
Ohinewai
Pukekapia
Lake Whaka
Mangawara
Orini
Pakitonga
Awaiti
Karangahake
Tirohia
Waitawheta
Waihou
Te Puninga
Taniwha
Waiti
Tahuna
Hoe-O-Tainui
Springdale
Otway
Elstow
Mangaiti
Te Puke
Waitoa
Shaftesbury
Manawaru
Te Aroha
Woodlands
Katikati
Tauranga Harbour
Waimata
Waitangaue
Kaimai Mamaku Forest Park
Matakana Island
Karewa Island
Matakana Island
Motiti Island
26

Hopuhopu
Huntly
Westmere
Taupiri
Komakorau
Ngaruawahia
Whitikahu
Tauhei
Mangateparu
Morrinsville
Waitoa
Hoe
Wairakau Mamaku Forest Park
Aongatete
Omokoroa Beach
Moturiki Island
1
45
47

3000 m+
2000–3000 m
1000–2000 m
500–1000 m
200–500 m
100–200 m
0–100 m

43

Hamilton and Central Plateau

The central North Island is a region of great geographic diversity. It has plains, rolling hills, mountains, lakes, volcanoes, forests, caves and a cold desert. There are pockets of intensively settled land, such as the areas around Hamilton, and expanses of landscape where there are virtually no settlements. The Volcanic Plateau is a region of active vulcanism, extending from National Park through to Rotorua. The Waikato region is drained by the North Island's largest river, while Lake Taupo is the largest lake in New Zealand. Hamilton (170,000), which lies astride the Waikato River, is New Zealand's largest inland city.

ACCOMMODATION

Novotel Tainui Hamilton: 7 Alma Street, Hamilton, tel: (07) 838 1366, fax: (07) 838 1367, freephone: 0800 450 050, e-mail: h2159-reoz@accor.com website: www.novotel.co.nz
Located right in the city's central business district.
Waitomo Caves Hotel: Lemon Point Road, RD7 Otorohanga, tel: (07) 878 8204, fax: (07) 878 8205, e-mail: info@waitomocaveshotel.co.nz

website: www.waitomocaveshotel.co.nz
A historic hotel, set above the Waitomo Caves village.
DeBretts Thermal Resort:
Taupo-Napier Highway, SH5, Taupo, tel: (07) 378 8559, fax: (07) 377 2181, e-mail: info@debrettsresort.co.nz website: www.debrettsresort.co.nz
The cabins and lodges of DeBretts Thermal Resort are adjacent to the thermal pools.

USEFUL CONTACTS

Hamilton i-SITE Visitor Centre:
cnr Bryce & Anglesea Streets, Hamilton, tel: (07) 839 3580.
Waikato District i-SITE Visitor Centre:
160 Great South Road, Huntly, tel: (07) 828 6406.
Otorohanga i-SITE Visitor Centre:
21 Maniapoto Street, tel: (07) 873 8951.
Waitomo Caves i-SITE Visitor Centre:
21 Waitomo Caves Road, tel: (07) 878 7640.
Websites: www.waikatonz.com
www.maungatrust.org
www.waitomo.co.nz
www.hobbitontours.com

Left: New Zealand's national bird, the flightless, nocturnal kiwi, can be seen at Otorohanga's Kiwi House. The kiwi is now a highly endangered species.

MAIN ATTRACTIONS

- See **kiwi** and other native **fauna and flora** at the **Kiwi House**, Otorohanga.
- Exploring the **limestone caves** at Waitomo, near Otorohanga.
- Browsing in the **antique shops** of Tirau and Cambridge.
- Visiting **Cambridge**, a very English country town with many mature deciduous trees.
- Taking a **paddle-steamer** on the Waikato River at Hamilton.
- **Surfing** at **Raglan**, on the west coast, one of New Zealand's premier board-riding locations.
- Soaking in **thermal pools** on the Volcanic Plateau.
- Driving across the Desert Road, from Turangi to Waiouru, and seeing the changing views of **Mounts Ruapehu, Ngauruhoe** and **Tongariro**.
- **Skiing** or **snowboarding** on Mount Ruapehu.

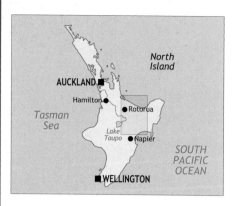

Rotorua and Bay of Plenty

The Bay of Plenty is one of New Zealand's most attractive and fastest-developing regions. The most recent census showed that in the last five years the population of the western Bay of Plenty had increased by 10.2%. The Bay consists of a long sweep of sandy coastline extending from Matakana Island in the north to Opotiki in the east, backed by a coastal plain which is among the most productive horticultural districts in the country. The plain is sheltered by the Kaimai Ranges, giving the Bay of Plenty high sunshine hours which is ideal for the growth and ripening of crops such as kiwifruit, avocados, tamarillos, citrus fruit and grapes.

MAIN ATTRACTIONS

- **Climbing** Mauao for superb **views** of Tauranga Harbour and the Bay of Plenty coastline.
- Experiencing a traditional Maori hangi and concert at **Tamaki Maori Village**, and browsing in the largest tribal marketplace in Rotorua.
- **Wine and culinary tasting** at local wineries Morton Estate and Mills Reef.
- Driving up to the **Minden Lookout** in Te Puna for fine views of the Bay.
- White-water rafting on one of the rivers which flow down from the Kaimai Range.
- **Swimming** with dolphins in the Bay.
- **Hiking** through the forests surrounding **Lake Waikaremoana**.

Right: *Pohutu Geyser, a main attraction in the Whakarewarewa Forest Park, Rotorua, is an impressive sight when it spouts steam.*

USEFUL CONTACTS

Tauranga i-SITE: 95 Willow Street, Tauranga, tel: (07) 578 8103, e-mail: tauranga@i-site.org
Mount Maunganui i-SITE: Salisbury Avenue, Mount Maunganui, tel: (07) 575 5099, e-mail: mtmaunganui@i-site.org
Katikati Information Centre: 36 Main Road, Katikati, tel: (07) 549 1658, e-mail: katikatinfo@wbopdc.govt.nz
Te Puke Information Centre: 130 Jellicoe Street, Te Puke, tel: (07) 573 9172, e-mail: tepukeinfo@wbopdc.govt.nz
Travel time: Driving from Auckland to Tauranga is 2 hours 55 minutes, flight time is 40 minutes.
Website: www.bayofplentynz.com
Tauranga Airport is just outside Mount Maunganui town, 3km across the harbour from the centre of Tauranga. There are regular flights from the airport to Auckland and Wellington, and shuttle connections to Tauranga city.

A **B** **C** **D**

1
2
3
4
5

45
49
53

East Coast and Poverty Bay

The East Coast is the most remote but also one of the loveliest regions of the North Island. It is one of the few regions where Maori still comprise the majority of the population. The drive from Opotiki east, along the Pacific Coast Highway, has vistas of sea, headlands and bays, most overlooked by pohutukawa trees. Inland is the rugged, forested Raukumara Range, which is crowned by Mount Hikurangi (1754m), which has the distinction of being the first place on Earth to receive the first rays of the new day's sun. The region's only city is Gisborne, which is located on an agriculturally rich lowland, misnamed Poverty Bay in 1769 by Captain James Cook.

MAIN ATTRACTIONS

- The **coastal drive** from Opotiki to Te Araroa along the **Pacific Coast Highway**.
- **Dining** at a waterfront restaurant overlooking **Gisborne's boat harbour**.
- The **view** to the north from the top of **Kaiti Hill**, overlooking the city of Gisborne.
- **Gisborne's surf beaches**, Wainui and Waikanae.
- Visiting the **wineries** in the Gisborne area and sampling the local speciality, chardonnay.
- Eastwoodhill **Aboretum tree and shrub collection**, about 35km from Gisborne.

Right: *Port and Waikanae Beach, Gisborne.*
Below: *A statue of Captain James Cook, overlooking Gisborne from Kaiti Hill. Cook and his expedition landed on the beach below the hill in October, 1769, the first Europeans to set foot on the shores of New Zealand.*

USEFUL CONTACTS

Locate the nearest local i-Site Visitor Information Centre and get the handy little booklet called 'Traveller's Guide to the Pacific Coast Highway'.
Opotiki i-SITE Visitor Centre:
cnr St John & Elliott Streets, Opotiki, tel: (07) 315 3031, fax: (07) 315 3032, e-mail: infocentre@odc.govt.nz
Gisborne i-SITE Visitor Information Centre: 209 Grey Street, Gisborne, tel: (06) 868 6139, fax: (06) 868 6138, e-mail: info@gisbornenz.com
website: www.gisbornenz.com
Wairoa i-SITE Information Centre:
cnr SH2 and Queen Street, Wairoa, tel: (06) 838 7440,
e-mail: weavic@xtra.co.nz
website: www.wairoanz.com

A B C D

1
2
3
4
5

Whangaparaoa
Orete Point
Waihau Bay
Raukokore
Papatea Bay
Papatea
Waikawa Point
Whanarua Bay
Wharekura Point
Te Kaha Point
Hariki Beach
Awanui
Waiorore
Omaio Bay
Pariokara
Otuwhare
Otehirinaki
Whitianga
Houpoto
Te Kaha
Rangipeua
▲ 1041 m

Otamaroa
Oruaiti Beach
Potaka
Hicks Bay
Matakaoa Point
Hicks Bay
Haupara Point
Tokata
Te Araroa
Horoera
Horoera Point
Awatere
East Cape
East Island
Maraehara
Rangitukia
Tikitiki
Waiomatatini

Karakatuwhero
Kopuapounamu
Poroporo
Maraehara

Raukumara
Forest Park
Puketoetoe
▲ 1120 m
Mangatutara
RAUKUMARA RANGE
Tamarara ▲ 1325 m
Waitahaia

Hikurangi
▲ 1754 m
Whakapourangi
Hiruharama
Aorangi
Kopuaroa
Takapau
Ihungia
Huiarua

Whakawhitira
Kakariki
Takamore
Ruatoria
Reporua
Mahora
Pohatukura
Tuparoa
Kaimoho Point
Wharenonga
Ohineakai
Waipiro Bay
Waipiro Bay
Te Puia Springs
Moutahiauru Island
Waima
Te Aruru
Koutunui Point
Tokomaru Bay
Ongaruru
Tokomaru Bay
Hikuwai
Mawhai Point

Takaputahi
Whakarau

Motu
Mangatu Forest
Waihaoa
Waiau
Arero
Tauwhareparae
Huanui
▲ 479 m
The Five Bridges
Mangatuna
Wharekaka
Takapau
Paremata

35
Anaura Bay
Motuoroi Island
Koutunui Head
Tokatea Rocks
Kaiaua Bay
Paerau Point
Tolaga Bay
Tolaga Bay
Hauiti
Pourewa Island

Whatatutu
Whataroa
Kanakanaia
Pakarae
Otoko
Puha
Te Karaka
Waimata
Rere
Waipaoa
Kaitaratahi
Eastwoodhill Aboretum ★
Ngatapa
▲ 493 m
Ormond
Waituhi
Waihirere
Pehiri
Patutahi
Hexton
Hangaroa
Matawhero
Manutuke
Waerengaokuri

Waihau Beach
Waihau Bay
35
Waiharehare Bay
Gable End Foreland
Gable Islet
Whangara
Whangara Island
Pariokonohi Point
Pouawa
Turihaua Point
Gisborne
Makorori
Okitu
Wainui
Tuaheni Point
Poverty Bay

Muriwai
Waingake
Young Nicks Head
Maraetaha
Bartletts
Wharerata Forest
Tukemokihi
2
Morere
Mahanga
Nuhaka
Kopuawhara
Opoutama
Oraka Beach
Mahia Beach
Whakatakahe Head
Mahia
Table Cape
Mahia Peninsula
Te Heruotaraia Point

N

53

3000 m+
2000–3000 m
1000–2000 m
500–1000 m
200–500 m
100–200 m
0–100 m

47

New Plymouth and Taranaki

The province of Taranaki is dominated by the dormant volcanic cone of Mount Taranaki (2518m) and its ring plain. Egmont National Park, surrounding the mountain, contains many hiking trails, and in suitable conditions, a summit climb. The province's coastline is also spectacular, from the White Cliffs of the North Taranaki Bight to the black sand beaches of South Taranaki. Surf Highway 45 is the name given to the coast road which links New Plymouth to Opunake, along which there are several famous windsurfing and board-riding locations. Between the coast and Mount Taranaki's forests are lush rolling pastures, devoted mainly to dairy farming.

MAIN ATTRACTIONS

- **Surf beaches** at Oakura and Opunake.
- **Climbing** the slopes of Mount Taranaki.
- **Strolling** through New Plymouth's **Pukekura Park** and adjoining **Brooklands Park**.
- **Walk** along New Plymouth's **coastal walkway**.
- **The Rhododendron Festival**: every October/November at **Pukeiti Gardens**.
- **Puke Ariki**, in New Plymouth, an integrated **museum, library** and **research centre**.
- The **walkway** at **White Cliffs**, in coastal North Taranaki.
- **Dairyland**, near Hawera, a gigantic **dairy factory** with displays of milk production.

Above: *Mount Taranaki/Egmont (2518m) and Egmont National Park, Taranaki.*
Left: *Coastal Walkway, New Plymouth.*

USEFUL CONTACTS

Website: www.taranaki.co.nz
Selected accommodation locations can be seen at the following website:
www.mttaranaki.co.nz
New Plymouth i-SITE Visitor Centre: Puke Ariki, 65 St Aubyn Street, New Plymouth, tel: (06) 759 6060, fax: (06) 759 6073, e-mail: info@newplymouth.govt.nz website: www.newplymouthnz.com
i-SITE South Taranaki: 55 High Street, Hawera, tel: (06) 278 8599, fax: (06) 278 6599, e-mail: visitorinfo@stdc.govt.nz
Stratford Visitor Information Centre: Prospero Place, Stratford, freephone: 0800 765 670, tel: (06) 765 6708, fax: (06) 765 6709, e-mail: info@stratford.govt.nz website: www.stratfordnz.co.nz

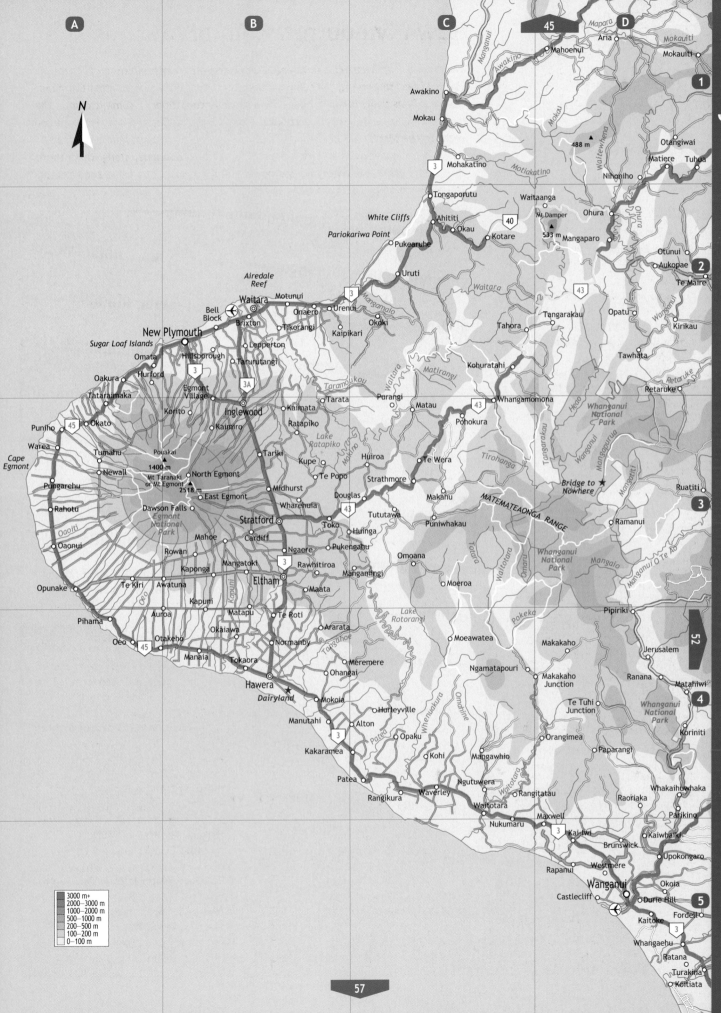

A   B   C   D

N

1

45   Mapara   Mokauiti

Aria
Mahoenui   Mokauiti

Manganui
Awakino   488 m   Otangiwai

Awakino   Mokau   Mokau   Matiere   Tuhua

Mohakatino   Nihoniho

3   Motiakatino

Tongaporutu   Waitaanga   Mt Damper   Ohura
White Cliffs   Ahititi   40   533 m   Mangaparo   Otunui
Pariokariwa Point   Okau   Kotare   Aukopae
Pukearuhe   Te Maire

Uruti   Waitara   43   Opatu
Airedale   Motunui   Tangarakau   Kirikau
Reef   Waitara   Onaero   Urenui   3   Tahora   Tawhata
Waitara   Bell   Okoki   Kohuratahi   Retaruke
Block   Brixton   Tikorangi   Kaipikari
New Plymouth   Lepperton   Matirangi   Whangamomona   Retaruke
Sugar Loaf Islands   Omata   Hillsborough   Tarurutangi   Taramoukou   Waitara   43   Whanganui
Oakura   Hurford   3   Korito   3A   Tarata   Purangi   Matau   43   National
Tataraimaka   Egmont   Inglewood   Kaimata   Pohokura   Park
Village   Kaimiro   Ratapiko   Lake   Heao   Tirohanga
Puniho   45   Okato   Pouakai   Ratapiko   Huiroa   Te Wera   MATEMATEAONGA RANGE
Warea   Tumahu   1400 m   Tariki   Kupe   Strathmore   Bridge to   Ruatiti
Cape   Newall   Mt Taranaki   North Egmont   Te Popo   Makahu   Nowhere
Egmont   Pungarehu   or Mt Egmont   2518 m   Midhurst   Douglas   Ramanui   3
Rahotu   Dawson Falls   East Egmont   Wharehuia   43   Tututawa   Whanganui
Oaonui   Egmont   Stratford   Toko   Huinga   Puniwhakau   National
National   Mahoe   Cardiff   Park   Totara
Park   Rowan   Ngaere   Pukengahu   Omoana   Moana
Opunake   Kaponga   Mangatoki   Rawhitiroa   Moeroa   Pipiriki
Te Kiri   Awatuna   3   Manganingi   Jerusalem
Pihama   Auroa   Kapuni   Matapu   Eltham   Maata   Moeawatea   Makakaho   Ranana
Oeo   45   Okaiawa   Te Roti   Lake   Makakaho   Matahiwi
Otakeho   Ararata   Rotorangi   Ngamatapouri   Junction
Manaia   Normanby   Te Tuhi   Whanganui
Tokaora   Meremere   Junction   National
Hawera   Ohangai   Makakaho   Park
Dairyland   Mokoia   Hurleyville   Junction   Koriniti
Manutahi   Alton   Orangimea   Paparangi   Whakaihuwhaka
Opaku   Mangawhio
Kakaramea   Kohi   Raoriaka
Patea   Ngutuwera   Rangitatau   Parikino
Rangikura   Waverley   Waitotara   Kaiwhaiki
Patea   Maxwell   Brunswick
Nukumaru   3   Kai-Iwi   Upokongaro
Westmere   Okoia
Rapanui   Wanganui
Castlecliff   Durie Hill   Fordell
Kaitoke   3
Whangaehu   Ratana
Turakina
Koitiata

1

2

3

4

5

45

52

3000 m+
2000–3000 m
1000–2000 m
500–1000 m
200–500 m
100–200 m
0–100 m

Hawke's Bay and Central North Island

Hawke's Bay is the North Island's largest and sunniest lowland. Its soil and climate are ideal for the growing of fruit and vegetables, hence the region's subtitle, the 'Fruit Bowl of New Zealand'. In recent years grape-growing and wine-making have become a major industry in Hawke's Bay, and the region has a well-earned reputation for its red wines, particularly merlot and cabernet sauvignon. Many of the wineries are open for tastings, meals and cellar door sales. Napier city is renowned for its Art Deco architecture, while there is also Spanish Mission architecture in Napier's sister city, Hastings — half an hour's drive south.

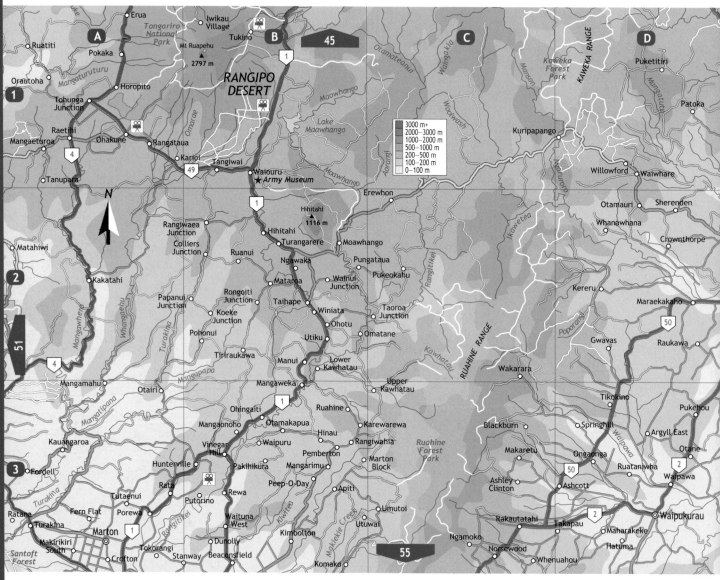

Above: *An Art Deco building, Napier.*

USEFUL CONTACTS

Domestic flights from the North Island's main centres to Napier take one hour.
Website: www.hawkesbay.com
Freephone: 0800 429 537.
Napier i-SITE Visitor Centre:
100 Marine Parade, Napier,
tel: (06) 834 1911, fax: (06) 835 7219
e-mail: info@napiervic.co.nz
Hastings i-SITE Visitor Centre: cnr Russell

& Heretaunga Streets, Hastings,
tel: (06) 873 5526, fax: (06) 873 5529,
e-mail: vic@hastingstourism.co.nz
Village Info Havelock North: at the
Roundabout, Havelock North,
tel: (06) 877 9600, fax: (06) 877 9601,
e-mail: info@villageinfo.co.nz
0800 HAWKES (0800 429 537) within
New Zealand.

USEFUL CONTACTS

Central Hawke's Bay Visitor Centre:
Railway Esplanade, Waipukurau,
tel: (06) 858 6488, fax: (06) 858 6489,
e-mail: chbinfo@xtra.co.nz
For Hawke's Bay events, visit the
website: www.hawkesbay.com/events
For accommodation, shopping, etc.,
visit the following website:
www.hawkesbaywinecountry.co.nz

MAIN ATTRACTIONS

- Touring the region's **wineries**, by coach, four-wheel-drive vehicle or bicycle.
- A trip overland or along the beach to the **Cape Kidnappers' gannet colony.**
- Watching the **sunrise** over one of the region's beaches, such as Whirinaki.
- Visit the **Hawke's Bay Museum**, in Napier, to view the exhibitions of the region's history.
- A **hot-air balloon** flight over Hawke's Bay.
- A leisurely **drive** through the horticultural districts of the **Esk Valley**, northwest of Napier.
- The **view** over the whole of Hawke's Bay from Te Mata Peak (399m), above Havelock North.

Wairarapa

The Wairarapa region is located in the southeast of the North Island. Largely a rural region, it is within easy reach by road and rail from Wellington. The Wairarapa has pastoral, mountain and coastal landscapes and a relaxed way of life. Pastoral farming has long been the basis of the region's economy, but in the last twenty-five years growing grapes for fine wines has contributed significantly to the Wairarapa's reputation. Its hot dry summers, cool winters and alluvial soils suit grape-growing admirably, pinot noir in particular. The charming, historic township of Martinborough is the centre of the wine-making district.

USEFUL CONTACTS

Tranz Metro connects Wellington city to the Wairarapa. For timetable information or to book, call free on 0800 471 227, website: www.tranzmetro.co.nz
websites: www.wairarapanz.com
www.classicwinetrail.co.nz
www.stonehenge-aotearoa.com
Masterton Visitor Centre:
316 Queen Street, Masterton,

tel: (06) 370 0900, fax: (06) 378 8451, e-mail: info@wairarapanz.com
Martinborough Visitor Centre:
18 Kitchener Street, Martinborough,
tel: (06) 306 9043, fax: (06) 306 8033,
e-mail: martinborough@wairarapanz.com
Drive time to the Wairarapa over the Rimutaka Range from Wellington is one hour and 10 minutes.

Above: *Cobblestone Village Museum, Greytown, on SH2 in the Wairarapa.*
Left: *Cape Palliser Lighthouse. The lighthouse stands on the North Island's southernmost point, near Black Rocks, at the extreme southeast of the Wairarapa region.*

MAIN ATTRACTIONS

- **The Mount Bruce National Wildlife Centre.**
- The **wine trails** around Martinborough township.
- The preserved **Victorian main street** of Greytown.
- **Stonehenge Aotearoa**, at Carterton.
- The **lighthouse** and **beaches** at **Castlepoint**.
- A **drive** to **Ngawi** to visit the **historic lighthouse** at **Cape Palliser**.
- The **hike** to the spectacular **Putangirua Pinnacles**.
- The three-day Tora **walk** through farmland and along the Wairarapa coast.
- **Tramping** in **Tararua Forest Park**, in the **Tararua Ranges**.

Wellington and Manawatu

This region is separated from the Wairarapa by a range of forested mountains, from the Rimutakas east of Wellington to the Tararua and Ruahine Ranges, east of the Manawatu plain. The west coast of the lower North Island is long and straight, with mostly windswept beaches backed by sand dunes and wetlands. The mighty island of Kapiti dominates the coastline from Te Horo to Raumati. Wellington city is supremely situated around its harbour, Port Nicholson, and is a compact, sophisticated city. Palmerston North, the hub of the Manawatu, lies just to the west of the gorge where the Manawatu River cuts through the mountain ranges.

MAIN ATTRACTIONS

- **Otari-Wilton's Bush:** a botanical reserve situated only minutes from the city.
- Hiking along the cliffs to enjoy the sea views at **Makara**, west of Wellington.
- **Hiking** from Eastbourne around the harbour to Pencarrow Head.
- Hiking along the many tracks through the **Tararua Range**.
- **Queen Elizabeth Park:** a regional park on the Kapiti coast.
- **Kapiti Island Nature Reserve:** A permit from the Department of Conservation is required before a visit to the island can be made.
- Visiting the **New Zealand Rugby Museum** in Palmerston North.

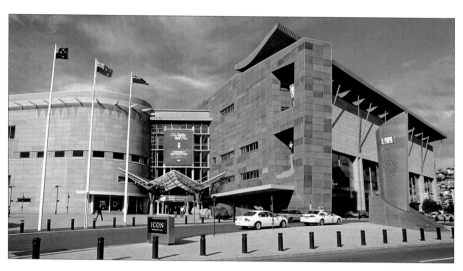

Above: *Museum of New Zealand – Te Papa Tongarewa houses displays and exhibitions.*
Below: *Kapiti Coast and Kapiti Island from Paekakariki Hill.*

USEFUL CONTACTS

Wellington City i-Site Visitor Centre, Civic Square:
tel: (04) 802 4860, fax: (04) 802 4863, e-mail: bookings@WellingtonNZ.com
website www.WellingtonNZ.com
Hutt City i-SITE Visitor Centre: The Pavilion, 25 Laings Road, Lower Hutt, tel: (04) 560 4715, fax: (04) 570 3374, e-mail: findit@huttcity.govt.nz
website: www.visithuttcity.org.nz
Upper Hutt i-SITE Visitor Centre: 84–90 Main Street, Upper Hutt, tel: (04) 527 2141, fax: (04) 527 9818, e-mail: upperhutt@i-site.org
website: www.upperhuttcity.com
Paraparaumu Visitor Centre: Coastlands Parade, SH1, Paraparaumu, tel/fax: (04) 298 8195, e-mail: paraparaumu@naturecoast.co.nz
website: www.naturecoast.co.nz
Manawatu i-SITE Visitor Centre: The Square, Palmerston North, tel: (06) 350 1922, fax: (06) 350 1929, e-mail: manawatu.visitor-info@xtra.co.nz
website: www.manawatunz.co.nz
For more information on the parks of greater Wellington, check this website: www.gw.govt.nz
Other websites: www.WellingtonNZ.com and www.wellingtonwaterfront.co.nz

A B 51 C D 54 Kiwitea

Scale
3000 m+
2000–3000 m
1000–2000 m
500–1000 m
200–500 m
100–200 m
0–100 m

N

Lake Alice
Santoft Forest
Santoft
Kakariki
Halcombe
Makino
Cheltenham
Almadale
Bulls
Ohakea
Mt Biggs
Maewa
1
Parewanui
Sanson
Feilding
Colyton
Hiwinui
Flock House
Carnarvon
Waitohi
Awahuri
Aorangi
Moana Roa Beach
Glen Oroua
Kopane
Kauwhata
Kairanga
Whakaronga
Tangimoana
Oroua Downs
Taikorea
54
Palmerston North
Himatangi Beach
Himatangi
Longburn
Himatangi
Massey University
Bainesse
Linton
Turitea
2
Foxton Beach
Foxton
Opiki
56
Nikau
Moutoa
Tokomaru
Waitarere
Shannon
57
Waiwera
Poroutawhao
Mangaore
Kakariki
Hukanui
Heatherlea
Nireaha
Newman
Hokio Beach
Ihakara
57
Rongokokako
Eketahuna
Levin
Putara
Waiwaka
Muhunoa
Ohau
Gladstone
Tararua Forest Park
Mt Bruce National Wildlife Centre
Kaiparoro
55
Waikawa Beach
Muhunoa East
Mt Dundas 1500 m
Mount Bruce
Manakau
Mauriceville West
Mauriceville
Otaki Beach
Otaki
Mitre 1571 m
2
Te Horo Beach
Mt Crawford 1462 m
Kopuaranga
Rangitumau
Te Horo
Otaki Forks
Mt Holdsworth 1470 m
Mikimiki
Opaki
3
Waikanae Beach
Waikanae
965 m
Kaituna
Masterton
Raumati Beach
Paraparaumu
Carrington
Waingawa
Raumati South
924 m
Clareville
Carterton
Maunganui 708 m
Dalefield
Te Whanga
Paekakariki
Cloustonville
Pakuratahi
Matarawa
Gladstone
Pukerua Bay
Pakuratahi Forks
Greytown
Papawai
Longbush
Te Rewarewa Point
The Plateau
Pakuratahi
Carterton
Ponatahi
Mana Island
Titahi Bay
Plimmerton
2
Featherston
Morrisons Bush
Green Point Rock Point
Pauatahanui
Judgeford
58
2
Pigeon Bush
Longbush
Porirua
Elsdon
Porirua East
Upper Hutt
53
Pipinui Point
Linden
Blue Mountains
Whitemans Valley
Martinborough
Tawa
Redwood
2
High Misty 710 m
Lake Wairarapa
Tablelands
Melling
Lower Hutt
Johnsonville
Kahutara
Ngakonui
Makara Beach
1
Petone
Dyerville
Ohau Pt
Somes/Matio Is.
Wainuiomata
Hinakura
Makara
Puketaha 767 m
Tuhitarata
Mt Adams 863 m
Karori
Museum of New Zealand – Te Papa Tongarewa
Pirinoa
Ruakokoputuna
Glendhu
WELLINGTON
Miramar
Seatoun
Eastbourne
Wharekauhau
Island Bay
Pencarrow Head
Lake Ferry
Whangaimoana
Tuturumuri
Sinclair Head
Tora
Manurewa Pt
Baring Head
Windy Pt
Aorangi Range
Orongorongo
Palliser Bay
Putangirua Pinnacles
Hauangi Forest Park
Turakirae Head
Te Humenga Pt
Ngawihi
Te Kaukau Pt
Te Raukauwhakamataku Pt
Fur Seal Colony
Cape Palliser
Rocky Pt

Cape Jackson
Waihi Point
Kempe Point
Anakakata Bay
Motuara Island
Cape Koamaru
The Brothers
Long Island
Arapawa Island
Perano Head
East Bay
East Head
West Head
Lucky Point
Bushy Point
Glasgow Bay
Rununder Point
Cape Terawhiti
Oteranga Bay
Oteranga Head
Karori Rock
Fitzroy Bay

Rimutaka Range
Rimutaka Forest Park

Tararua Range
Tararua Forest Park

Otaki
Waiotauru
Waiohine
Tauherenikau

Whangaehu
Ruamahanga
Dry
Ruakokoputuna
Awhea
Opouawe
Otakaha Stream
Orongorongo
Oterei

Kapiti Island Nature Reserve and Marine Reserve
Kapiti Island

Cook Strait
Oharu Bay

4

5

61

Cape Campbell

57

Cape Farewell and Tasman Bay

This region in the extreme northwest of the South Island is one of the most beautiful in New Zealand. Featuring a long coastline with golden sand beaches, backed by fertile lowlands and forested mountains, the region also has vineyards, orchards, nature reserves and one of the most popular national parks in New Zealand, the Abel Tasman. Driving from Motueka over the steep Takaka hill road and down into Golden Bay is like entering a very different and beguiling world, one of valleys, farmland, estuaries, the great sweep of Golden Bay and the very northern tip of the South Island, Farewell Spit, which is a reserve for migratory birds.

Above: *A gannet colony at Farewell Spit. The spit, a long, sickle-shaped landform enclosing Golden Bay, is the protected habitat of several species of wading and migratory birds, including gannets, terns and godwits.*

Left: *Abel Tasman National Park, a 23,000-hectare area of forested mountains, coastal lagoons and gold-sand beaches. Hiking and sea kayaking are popular pursuits in the park.*

MAIN ATTRACTIONS

- **Hiking** and **kayaking** in **Abel Tasman National Park.**
- **Walking** along the **Heaphy Track** from the Aorere Valley across to the West Coast.
- A **four-wheel-drive** trip along to the **Farewell Spit Nature Reserve.**
- The **Ngarua Caves** and **Harwood's Hole**, on the Takaka Hill.
- **Waikoropupu (Pupu) Springs,** just outside Takaka.
- Shopping for **local arts and crafts** in Takaka township.
- **The Mussel Inn**, an atmospheric country pub outside Takaka.
- The pretty harbourside settlement of **Mapua**, with its many **cafés and craft shops.**

A B C D

N

Map Scale Legend
- 3000 m+
- 2000–3000 m
- 1000–2000 m
- 500–1000 m
- 200–500 m
- 100–200 m
- 0–100 m

Cape Farewell
Pilch Point
Puponga Farm Park
Bird Sanctuary
Farewell Spit
Ngaroa Bay
Puponga
Port Puponga
Puponga Point
Farewell Spit Nature Reserve
Bar Point
South Head Cone
Seaford
Pakawau
Sharks Head
Waikato
Mangarakau
Knuckle Hill 506 m
Golden Bay
Paturau River
Ferntown
Ruataniwha Inlet
Anatori
Lake Otuhie
Collingwood
Whanganui Inlet
Aorere
Milnthorpe
Parapara
Rockville
Bainham
Onekaka
Patons Rock
Taupo Point
Separation Point
Kahurangi Point
60
Puramahoi
Rangihaeata Head
Anapai Bay
Otukoroiti Point
Rangihaeata
Tarakohe
Totaranui
Rocks Point
Big Bay
Waitapu
Pohara
Awaroa Bay
Steep Point
Mackay Downs
Parapara Peak 1248 m
Takaka
Motupipi
Awaroa Head
Wekakura Point
Wakamarama Range
Waikoropupu Springs
Abel Tasman National Park
Tonga Island
Whakapoai Point
Kahurangi National Park
Kotinga
South Head
North Head
Pitt Head
Heaphy Bluff
Tubman Range
Mt Inaccessible 1495 m
Haupiri Ra
Hamama
East Takaka
Mt Evans 1156 m
Adele Island
Fisherman Island
Iwituaroa Ra
Heaphy Track
Gouland Range
Devil River Peak 1784 m
Marahau
Mid Point
Mt Ross 1309 m
Douglas Ra
Lake Stanley
Uruwhenua
Upper Takaka
Ngarua Caves
Kaiteriteri
Gunner Downs
Tasman Mountains
Waingaro
Lockett Range
Riwaka
Tasman Bay
Kohaihai Bluff
Lake Henderson
Brooklyn
Motueka
Port Motueka
Cobb Reservoir
Hoary Head 1473 m
Lower Moutere
Mariri
Glenduan
Wakapuaka
Oparara
Grindley Ridge
Morgan Range
Marshall Range
Grange Ridge
Mt Peel 1654 m
Pangatotara
Braeburn
Kina
Tasman
Boulder Bank
Marybank
Karamea
Market Cross
Umere
Arapito
Fenian Range
Garibaldi Ridge
Pokororo 1609 m
Ngatimoti
Harakeke
Moutere Bluff
Ruby Bay
Mapua
Wearable Arts Museum
Kongahu
Herbert Range
Arthur Range
The Twins 1796 m
Woodstock
Upper Moutere
Mahana
Bronte
Nelson
Thorpe
Dovedale
Redwood Valley
Stoke
Little Wanganui
Te Namu
Mt Kendall 1762 m
1592 m
Stanley Brook
Richmond
Hope
Mt Fugel 1374 m
Kahurangi National Park
Wangapeka
Matariki
Rakau
Tapawera
Brightwater
Spring Grove
60
6
Kongahu Point
Radiant Range
Mt Webb 1350 m
Little Wanganui
Wakefield
Wai-iti
Mt Stewart 1278 m
Corbyvale
Tadmor
Mararewa
Foxhill
Belgrove
Mt Richmond Forest Park
Motupiko
Kohatu
Lake Cholice
Summerlea
Nikau
Mokihinui
Mokihinui
Mt Misery 1383 m
Mt Owen 1876 m
Lookout Range
Tui
Korere
Kaka
Miko
Matiri Range
Gordon Range
Hope Range
Golden Downs
Red Hill 1790 m
Mt Patriarch 1656 m
Hector
67
Ben Murray 1440 m
Atapo
63
Ngakawau
Stockton
Millerton
Granity
Glenhope
Mt Vaughan 1176 m
Owen River
Kawatiri
Howard Junction
Mt Phillips 1542 m
Lyell Range
Owen Junction
Blue Cliffs Ridge
New Creek
Newton Flat
Longford
Howard
Tophouse
63
Lyell
6
Ariki
Murchison
Noels Peak 1013 m
Rotoroa
St Arnaud
Inangahua Junction
Glengarry
Mangles Valley
Tutaki
Lake Rotoiti
Berlins
Inangahua
Boundary Peak 1218 m
Shenandoah
Raglan Range
Inangahua Landing
65
Six Mile
Lake Rotoroa
Travers
Nelson Lakes National Park
69
Victoria Forest Park
Paenga
1813 m
St Arnaud Range
Rotokohu
Larrys Creek
Matakitaki
Upper Matakitaki
Elise Peak 1807 m
Saxton 2044 m
Shingle Peak 2088 m

1
2
61
3
6
4
67
5

65 67

59

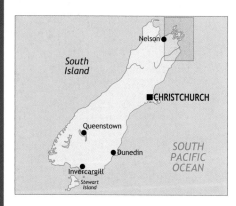

Marlborough

Marlborough is the largest wine-producing region in New Zealand, with eighty vineyards producing 40 per cent of New Zealand's wine output, in particular sauvignon blancs and bottle-fermented sparkling wines. The region's high sunshine hours — on average 2600 annually — and well-drained soils comprise a terroir which is ideal for the growth and ripening of white wine grapes. Marlborough is also the gourmet capital of the South Island. Along with its fine wines, the region is also famous for seafoods such as salmon, crayfish, scallops and green-lipped mussels, which thrive in the pure waters of the Marlborough Sounds.

MAIN ATTRACTIONS

- **Exploring** the foreshore of **Picton** town and the **Picton Museum**.
- **Cruising** the channels and bays of the **Sounds** on a **chartered boat**.
- **Diving** in the clear waters of the Long Island Marine Reserve.
- Sampling Marlborough's great **sauvignon blancs** and **seafood**.
- Following the **Marlborough Art and Craft Trail**.
- Participating in a **Marlborough Culinary School** session.
- Staying at one of the **secluded lodges** in the Marlborough Sounds.
- **Hiking** or **biking (cycling)** along some of the Sounds' many **scenic trails**.

Above: *A typically tranquil bay and beach near Picton in the Marlborough Sounds.*
Left: *Highfield Estate, one of the Marlborough region's many stylish wineries.*

USEFUL CONTACTS

Blenheim i-SITE Visitor Centre:
Blenheim Railway Station, Blenheim, tel: (03) 577 8080, fax: (03) 577 8079, e-mail: blenheim@i-SITE.org
Picton i-SITE Visitor Centre:
Picton Foreshore, tel: (03) 520 3113, fax: (03) 573 5021,
e-mail: picton@i-SITE.org
Flight times to Blenheim: from Auckland, one hour and 20 minutes; from Wellington 25 minutes; from Christchurch 50 minutes.
Daily air shuttles between Blenheim and Nelson, Wellington and Paraparaumu, freephone: 0800 777 000, website: www.air2there.com
Other websites:
www.destinationmarlborough.com
www.wine-marlborough-festival.co.nz
www.marlborough.artnz.com
www.marlboroughtravel.co.nz
www.soundsconnection.co.nz

A   B   C   D

N

1

Stephens
Island
Cape Stephens   Saddle Rocks
Victory
Nile Head   Island
Bottle Point   Patuki   Whakaterepapanui Island
Rangitoto Islands
D'Urville Island   Mukahanga   Jag Rocks
Greville   Old Mans Head
Harbour   Half Way Point
Ragged Point   Attempt Hill   Trio Islands
729 m
Haukawakawa   D'Urville   Nukuwaiata   Te Kakaho Island
Peninsula   Island
Paddock   French   Chetwode Islands
Rocks   Pass   Culdaff Point
Sauvage Point   Te Akaroa   Titi Island
Current Basin   Forsyth   Cape
Reef   Island   Lambert   Cape Jackson
Papawai Bay   Mt Shewell   Point   Waihi Point
776 m   Marlborough Sounds   Port Gore
Maritime Park   Kempe Point
Otuhaereroa Island   Elaine   Maud   Beatrix   Black
Cape Soucis   Bay   Island   Bay   Head   Anakakata Bay
Croisilles   Tawhitinui Reach   Te Rewarewa Point
Pukerau Point   Harbour   Tawero   Endeavour   Motuara   Cape Koamaru   Plimmerton
Grahams Point   Point   Inlet   Island   Mana Island   Titahi
Whangamoa   Mt Stokes   Bay
Head   Mt Stanley   1203 m   Long   The Brothers   Green Point
Manaroa   Island   Rock Point   Elsdon
Pepin   Delaware Bay   Okiwi Bay   971 m   Porirua
Island   Tennyson   Crail Bay   Arapawa   Pipinui Point   Tawa
Inlet   Waitaria   Kenepuru   Island   Redwood   Linden
Glenduan   Bay   Head   Perano Head   Makara Beach   Johnsonville
Wakapuaka   Nopera   Blumine   Ohau Pt   Museum of New Zealand
Hira   Te Mahia   Island   East Head   Makara   Te Papa Tongarewa
West Head   Karori
Rai Valley   Carluke   Curious   Tarakawa   Cape Terawhiti   WELLINGTON   Miramar
Mt Rutland   Wedge   Cove   575 m   Lucky Point   Oteranga Bay   Island   Seatoun
1008 m   Point   Bushy Point   Bay
Havelock   Anakiwa   Waikawa   Glasgow Bay   Oteranga Head   248 m
Pelorus   Canvastown   Ferry   Rununder Point   Karori Rock   Pencarrow
Bridge   Terminal   Picton   Karaka Bay   Sinclair   Head
995 m   Linkwater   Robertson Point   Head   Fitzroy Bay
6   Mt Pleasant   Baring Head
Koromiko
Mt Cullen   Para   Cloudy Bay
1055 m   Rarangi
1   Tuamarina
Okaramio   Spring   Marshlands
Kaituna   Creek   Wairau Pa
Mt Richmond   Rapaura   Grovetown
Forest Park   Renwick   Blenheim
952 m   Woodbourne   6   Wairau Bar
Te Rou   Fairhall   Riverlands
Cobb Cottage
63   White Bluffs
Wairau
Valley
Hillersden   Dashwood
Devils Backbone   Blind
1188 m   Seddon   River   Clifford Bay
Mt Phillips   Lake Grassmere   Mussel Point
1542 m   Jack   Altimarloch   Lake   Cape Campbell
1306 m   Mt Horrible   Grassmere
Pudding Hill   1579 m   Welds   Hauwai
1464 m   Big Bolton   Hill   Taimate
Camden   1457 m   Long Point
Mt Misery   Peggioh   Ward
Mt Elliott   1080 m   1052 m   Mirza
1512 m   Gladstone   Isolated Hill   Needles Point
Kilgram
Te Rapa
Langridge   Crows Nest   The Pikes   Wharanui
Middlehurst   Mitre Peak   2480 m   1190 m
2621 m   67
Kekerengu

2

59

57

3

4

5

3000 m+
2000–3000 m
1000–2000 m
500–1000 m
200–500 m
100–200 m
0–100 m

61

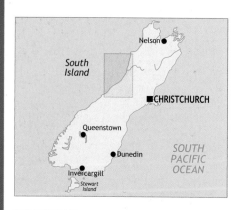

West Coast

The West Coast of the South Island has a unique set of geographical features which make it an ideal region for those who love adventurous pursuits. 'The Coast' as it is commonly known consists of a very long, narrow coastal plain which is always in sight of the saw-toothed Southern Alps. Between the coast and the mountains are stands of native forest, while a number of swift-flowing rivers pour down from the Alps, across the narrow plain and into the Tasman Sea. In the central part of the Coast are the towns founded on gold- and coal-mining: Westport, Greymouth and Hokitika, while in the south are two mighty glaciers, Fox and Franz Josef.

MAIN ATTRACTIONS

- **Walking** along the three- to five-day Heaphy Track.
- The **limestone caves** and formations of the **Oparara Basin**.
- **Rafting** on one of the Coast's tumbling rivers.
- **Dining** on whitebait fritters.
- **Kayaking** on the Hokitika River.
- Visiting one of the region's **five national parks**.
- Visiting the **Coaltown Museum** in Westport, and the remains of the **coal-mining** community of Denniston (*see* map p. 65).
- **Fishing for trout** in Lake Brunner and its tributaries.
- Taking the **Fox Glacier Valley Walk**.
- A **guided tour** of the Okarito Lagoon.

Top left: *Fox Glacier is one of the top visitor attractions on New Zealand's unique West Coast.*

Bottom left: *Knights Point, just before heading inland to Haast Pass. The shoreline of 'the Coast' is exposed to prevailing winds from the Tasman Sea.*

USEFUL CONTACTS

Reefton Visitor i-SITE: 67 Broadway, Reefton, tel: (03) 732 8391, fax: (03) 732 8616, e-mail: reeftoninfo@xtra.co.nz website: www.reefton.co.nz
Westland Visitor Information Centre: Carnegie Complex, cnr Hamilton and Tancred Streets, Hokitika, tel: (03) 755 6166, fax: (03) 755 5011, e-mail: hkkvin@xtra.co.nz
The West Coast is 550km from north to south, so although the main roads are of a good standard, it's best not to rush a visit to the region. Allow several days to sample the natural and cultural attractions of the long narrow region known as 'the Coast'.

Tasman Sea

A B C D

N

Scale (elevation):
3000 m+
2000–3000 m
1000–2000 m
500–1000 m
200–500 m
100–200 m
0–100 m

Charleston

65

1

Kaipakati Point
Tiromoana

6

Perpendicular Point
Dolomite Point
Pancake Rocks and Blowholes
Punakaiki

Mt Bovis 1252 m

Paparoa National Park

PAPAROA RANGE

Fox
Pororari
Punakaiki
Rough
Waitakere
Ohikanui

Hawera 1190 m

Barrytown

2

Craigieburn
Totara Flat
Ahaura
Matai
Nelson Creek
Ngahere

Greigs
Motukiekie Rocks

6

Roa
Atarau
Blackball

7

Grey

Rapahoe
Point Elizabeth
Runanga
Cobden
Taylorville
Kamaka
Notown
Omoto
Stillwater

Greymouth
Karoro
Kaiata
Dobson
Kokiri
Kaimata

South Beach
Boddytown

Paroa
Rutherglen
Mining Town Replica (Shantytown)
Kotuku
Bell Hill
Aratika

Gladstone
Cameron
Dunganville
Marsden
Moana

Kangaroo Lake

Kumara Junction

Lake Brunner

Te Kinga
Lady Lake

3

Chesterfield
Kumara
Greenstone
Mitchells
Ruberslaw 1166 m
Rotomanu

Awatuna
Stafford
Dillmanstown
Lake Poerua
Poerua

6

Kaihinu
Goldsborough
Taramakau
Hohonu

73

Arahura

Hokitika
Takutai
Kaniere
Humphreys
Turiwhate
Wainihinihi
Jacksons
Aickens

73

Mananui
Woodstock

Ruatapu
Lake Mahinapua
Lake Kaniere
Arahura

Otira Lookout (Otira Viaduct)

Kokatahi

Styx

Mt Lancelot 2106 m

Kowhitirangi

Arthur's Pass

4

Ross
Historic Gold Town

Doctor Hill 686 m

Arthur's Pass National Park

73

Kakapotahi
Fergusons

Mt Ross 1798 m
Mt Greenlaw 2294 m

Bealey

Pukekura

Mt Browne 1366 m
Mt Findlay 1806 m

BLACK RANGE

Wanganui Bluff

Waitaha

Mt Bryce 2235 m
Mistake Hill 2095 m
Thesis Peak 2037 m

Craigieburn Forest Park

BIRDWOOD RANGE

Saltwater Lagoon
Whanganui
Lake Ianthe

Mt Marion 2118 m
ROLLESTON RANGE

Herepo

6

Mt Beaumont 2141 m

Mt Oakdan 1615 m

Abut Head
Kotuku (White Heron) Sanctuary

Mt Allen 1518 m

Mt Whitcombe 2644 m

RAGGED RANGE

Okarito Lagoon
Rotokino

SMYTH RANGE

Whitcombe
Mathias
Moa

Lake Coleridge

Okarito

Lake Wahapo
Te Taho

Speculation Hill 1387 m

Blair Peak 2495 m

Mt Medhurst 1961 m

5

Whataroa

WILBERG RANGE

Mt Adams 2223 m

Rakaia

Westland Tai Poutini National Park

The Forks

6

Newton Peak 2545 m
Mt Barlow 2088 m

Amazon Peak 2507 m
Mt Arrowsmith 2795 m

Lagoon Peak
Black Hill 2046 m

Lake Coleridge

Lake Mapourika
Tatare
Franz Josef

Perth
SOUTHERN ALPS

73

71

63

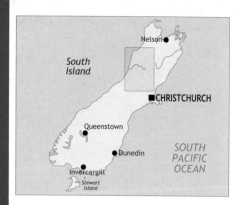

Arthur's Pass and Lewis Pass

The Southern Alps, the backbone of the South Island, can be driven through in three places: Lewis Pass, Arthur's Pass and Haast Pass. All three offer spectacular scenery along the way, but the approaches to Lewis Pass and Arthur's Pass, and the passes themselves, have some special attractions. For example, near the gateway to Lewis Pass is Hanmer Springs and Hanmer Forest Park. The first bathhouse here was built in 1883, and today Hanmer is a spa town. On the eastern side of the pass there are dry beech and tawhai forests; on the much wetter western slopes there is mixed podocarp rainforest and red-flowering rata trees.

MAIN ATTRACTIONS

- Soaking in the **thermal pools** at **Maruia Springs**, Lewis Pass.
- Enjoy the therapeutic waters at **Hanmer Springs Thermal Pools and Spa** (*see* map p. 67). • The **mountain views** from **Lewis Pass Lookout**, a clearing in the beech forest.
- One of the **day walks** which begin at **Arthur's Pass village**.
- The alpine scenery observed from the comfort of the **TransAlpine Express**.
- The spectacular **Pancake Rocks** at **Punakaiki**.

USEFUL CONTACTS

Arthur's Pass Visitor Centre/ Department of Conservation:
Main Road SH73, Arthur's Pass Village, tel: (03) 318 9211,
fax: (03) 318 9210,
e-mail: arthurspassvc@doc.govt.nz
website: www.doc.govt.nz/Explore/ 001~National-Parks/Arthurs-Pass-National-Park
Website: www.hanmersprings.co.nz

Right: Cape Foulwind, so named by Captain James Cook as he sailed up the West Coast in adverse conditions in 1769.
Below: Lake St James, Lewis Pass.

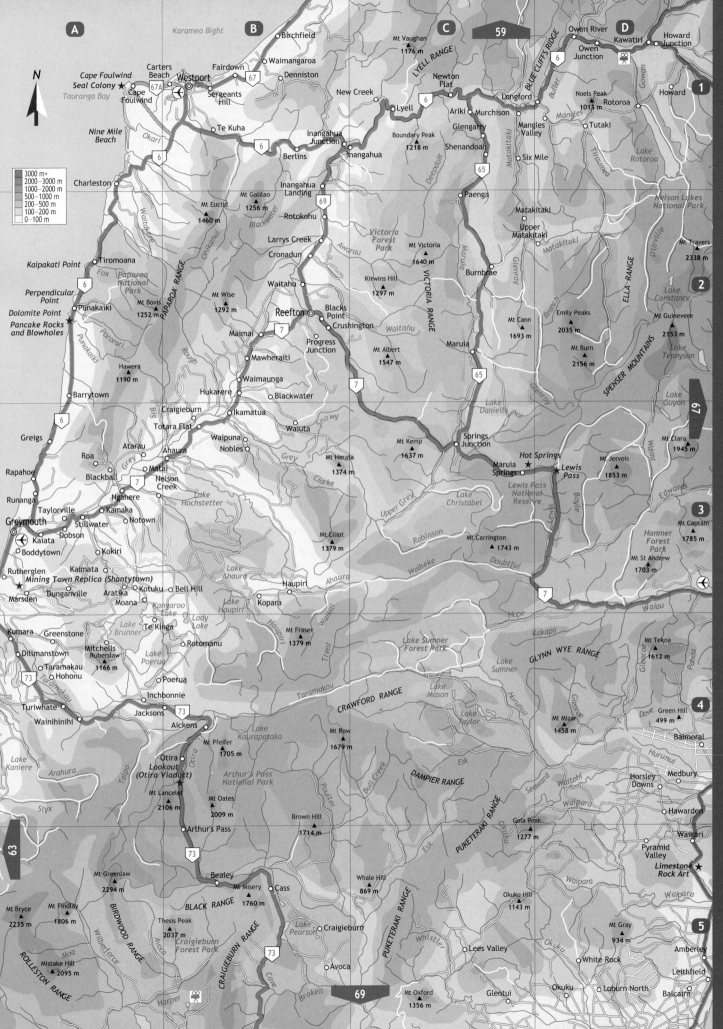

Kaikoura and Coast

An hour's drive south from Blenheim, along the coast on SH1, the Seaward Kaikoura Range comes into focus. Further south a road branches off SH1 and onto the Kaikoura Peninsula, where Kaikoura township is located. In the unusually deep waters surrounding the peninsula very cold waters from Antarctica mix with warm waters from the north and east, creating a rich food chain for fish, marine mammals and sea birds. Just off the peninsula it is possible to observe sperm whales, fur seals, as well as dolphins, from specially designed chartered vessels. Hence Kaikoura is known as 'Marine Watch Town'.

MAIN ATTRACTIONS

- The half-day **walking track** around the Kaikoura Peninsula.
- An **adventure tour** in the Clarence Valley, between Blenheim and Kaikoura.
- **Watching whales** and **seals** off the Kaikoura Peninsula.
- A **fishing charter trip** off the Kaikoura Peninsula.
- Sampling the **local seafood** in a Kaikoura restaurant.
- Tasting the local wine at the **winery** atop a cliff south of Kaikoura.
- Visiting the **Kaikoura Museum** to learn of the peninsula's Maori history and the role whaling played in Kaikoura's past.
- A **scenic flight** over the Kaikoura Peninsula and nearby mountain ranges.

Above: *A whale's flukes break the sea's surface just off the Kaikoura Peninsula, a popular whale-watching site.*
Below: *Kaikoura town and the Seaward Kaikoura Range.*

USEFUL CONTACTS

Kaikoura i-SITE Visitor Centre:
Westend, Kaikoura, tel: (03) 319 5641,
fax: (03) 319 6819,
e-mail: info@kaikoura.co.nz

website: www.kaikoura.co.nz
More websites:
www.kaikouranet.co.nz/fishing.htm
www.encounterkaikoura.co.nz

A   59   B   C   61   D

Howard Junction
Kikiwa
Tophouse
Howard
St Arnaud
63
1813 m

Devils Backbone
1188 m
Mt Phillips
1542 m
Jack
1306 m
Avon
Mt Horrible
1579 m
Altimarloch
Welds Hill
Seddon
Blind River
Lake Grassmere
Hauwaio
1
Taimate

RAGLAN RANGE
Wairau
Branch
Waihopai
Spray
Grey
Pudding Hill
1464 m
Big Bolton
1457 m
Camden
Mt Misery
1080 m
Peggioh
1052 m
Isolated Hill
Mirza
Kilgram
Te Rapa
Wharanui

Lake Rotoiti
Nelson Lakes National Park
ST ARNAUD RANGE
Travers Range
Elise Peak
1807 m
Saxton
2044 m
RAGLAN RANGE
Shingle Peak
2088 m
Langridge
Middlehurst
Acheron
Mt Elliott
1512 m
Gladstone
Mitre Peak
2621 m
Crows Nest
2480 m
The Pikes
1190 m
Kekerengu
2

Mt Travers
2338 m
Rainbow
Severn
Saxton
Molesworth
Awatere
INLAND KAIKOURA RANGE
Parikawa

Lake Constance
Mt Guinevere
2153 m
Mt Tarndale
1774 m
Alma
Acheron
Lake McRae
Mt Jackson
1525 m
Gridiron
1036 m
Clarence
Clarence
George Spur
2311 m
Clarence
Lake Tennyson
Mt Sebastopol
2013 m
BODDINGTON RANGE
Manakau
2610 m
Rakautara
Half Moon Bay
1

Lake Guyon
Mt Clara
1945 m
65
Clarence
Mt Giles
1857 m
Dillon
Clarence
SEAWARD KAIKOURA RANGE
Mt Fyffe
1602 m
Mangamaunu
Hapuku
1

Edwards
Acheron
Hawk Hills
Swyncombe
Mt Furneaux
70
Lynton Downs
Kahutara
Maori Leap Caves
Mt Fyffe
Whale and Dolphin Watching
Kaikoura
3

Mt Captain
1785 m
Chalwell
Peketa
Kowhai
South Bay
Kaikoura Peninsula

Hanmer Forest Park
Thermal Springs
Hanmer Springs
Mt Peter
990 m
Conway
Leader
965 m
Oaro
Goose Bay

Hanmer
70
Hundalee
Claverley

7
Waiau
Mason
Ferniehurst
1
Conway Flat
4

Pahau
Waiau
Rotherham
Hawkswood
Green Hill
499 m
Culverden
AMURI PLAIN
Waiau
Parnassus
Spotswood
Phoebe

Balmoral
Mt Ellen
419 m
Leamington
Caverhill
Mina
Cheviot
7
Medbury
Hurunui
Horsley Downs
Beckenham Hills
Ethelton
Domett
1
Gore Bay
Port Robinson
Hawarden
Greta
Hurunui Mouth

Waikari
Scargill
Waikari
Pendle Hill
530 m
Mana Island
5
Limestone Rock Art
Omihi
1
Greta Valley

Waipara
Waipara
Motunau Beach
Motunau Island

Glasnevin
Amberley
Leithfield
Amberley Beach
Balcairn
Leithfield Beach

N

3000 m+
2000–3000 m
1000–2000 m
500–1000 m
200–500 m
100–200 m
0–100 m

69

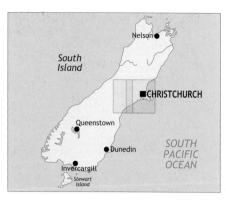

Christchurch and Banks Peninsula

Christchurch, the second largest city in New Zealand, lies on the eastern edge of the Canterbury Plains and is known as The Garden City. Built in the 1840s, the city has many neo-Gothic stone buildings, a central square where the cathedral is located, as well as fine parks and gardens. The city has spread south to the hills of Banks Peninsula, an extinct volcano deeply indented by two fine harbours, Lyttelton and Akaroa. Lyttelton, a 20-minute drive away, is Christchurch's port; Akaroa, a picturesque town two hours by road from the city around Banks Peninsula, was founded by French immigrants in the 1840s and retains a Gallic flavour.

Above: *Punting on the willow-lined River Avon, which meanders through Christchurch city's public parks and gardens.*

MAIN ATTRACTIONS

- Wandering through Christchurch's **Botanic Gardens**.
- Visiting the **Canterbury Museum**.
- Taking a walk, drive or bike ride along the **Port Hills**.
- Sampling the **fare** at one of Lyttelton's street cafés.
- Exploring the seaside villages of **Sumner** and **New Brighton**.
- Tasting the **wines** of the **Waipara Valley**, in North Canterbury.
- **Dining** at one of Akaroa's fine restaurants.
- Taking the **Akaroa walk** around the rim of an extinct volcano and savouring the coastal views.

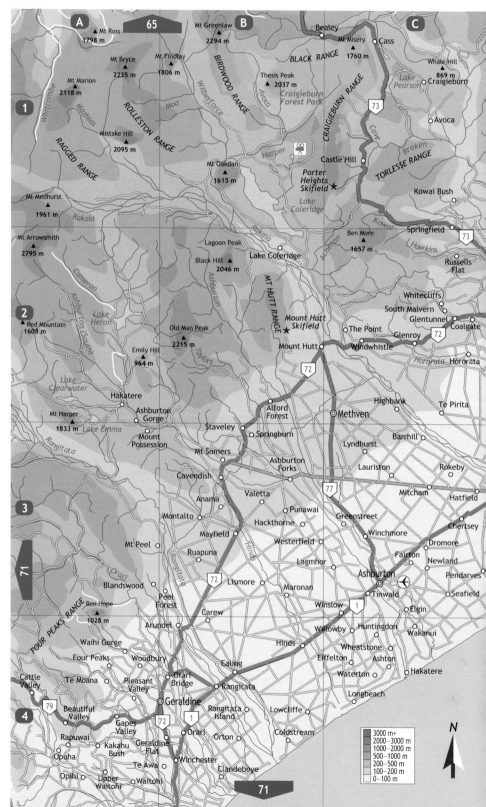

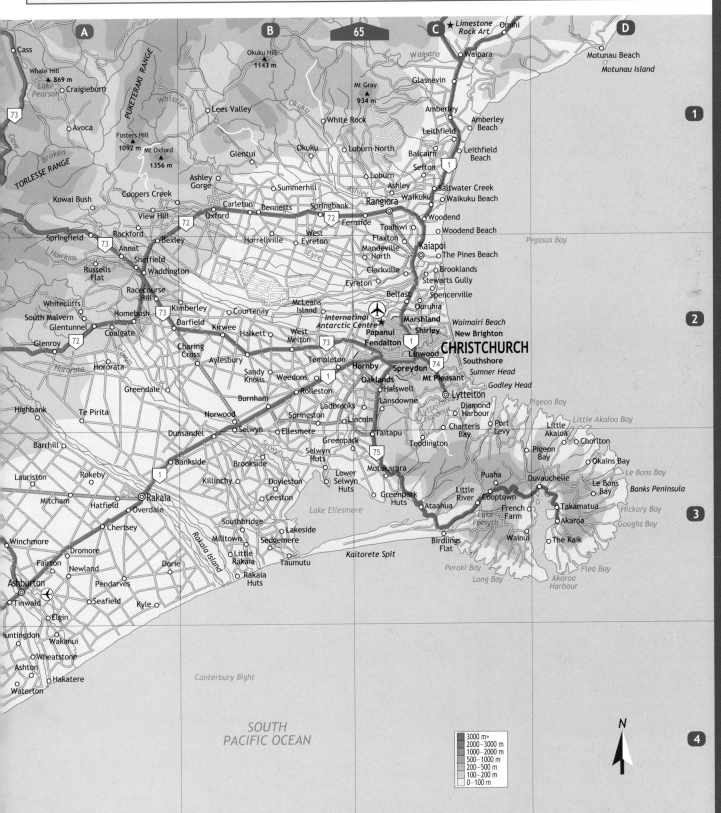

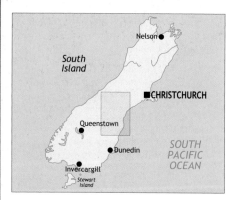

South Canterbury

Canterbury, New Zealand's largest lowland, extends from coastal Banks Peninsula to the foothills of the Southern Alps. The plains comprise a patchwork of mixed farmland and pine plantations, and from them on a clear day the Southern Alps are a constant presence along the western horizon. Inland Canterbury is a region of mountain grandeur — undulating downlands, high country tussock lands, dramatic gorges and braided, snow-fed rivers. There are ten skifields within a two and a half hour drive from Christchurch city, including two of New Zealand's best, Mount Hutt and Porter Heights.

MAIN ATTRACTIONS

- **Skiing** and **snow-boarding** at Mount Hutt or Porter Heights, Jul–Oct.
- Driving the **Inland Scenic Route 72**, from Darfield in the north to Geraldine in the south.
- Taking a **jet-boat ride** on one of Canterbury's braided rivers, such as the Waimakariri.
- Catch a **hot-air balloon ride** across the Canterbury Plains.
- **Hiking** the **Waimate Walkway**, for breathtaking views over South Canterbury.
- **Fishing** for salmon on the Rangitata and Waitaki Rivers.
- **Bird-watching** for rare NZ wet-land birds in **Ahuriri Conservation Park** and **Ben Avon Wetlands**.

Left: *Lodges and chairlift at Mount Hutt Skifield, Canterbury. A shuttle bus service connects Methven with the skifield. The field itself is nestled inside the eastern rim of the Southern Alps, and is one hour's drive from Christchurch. This skifield has New Zealand's longest ski season, from June to late October. It has a vertical rise of 672m.*

USEFUL CONTACTS

Methven i-SITE Visitor Centre: 121 Main Street, Methven, tel: (03) 302 8955, fax: (03) 302 8954, e-mail: info@methveninfo.org website: www.methveninfo.co.nz
Timaru i-SITE Visitor Information Centre: 2 George Street, Timaru, tel: (03) 688 6163, fax: (03) 684 0202, e-mail: info@timaru.com
Selwyn District: tel: (03) 324 8080, fax: (03) 324 3531, website: www.selwyndistrict.co.nz
For **Adventure Tours** in Christchurch and Canterbury, freephone: 0800 345 346, e-mail: info@adventuretours.com website: www.nzadventuretours.com

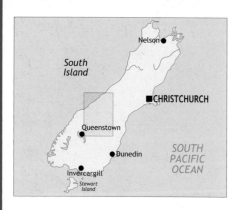

Aoraki/Mount Cook and Southern Alps

This region contains some of the most spectacular scenery in New Zealand, including Aoraki/Mount Cook (3754m), the country's highest peak, the Tasman Glacier and the lonely beauty of the Mackenzie Country. Mighty glaciers, turquoise glacial lakes, snow-capped mountains and scree-covered valley slopes — all soaked in dazzlingly clear light — make this region a delight to travel through at any time of year. The Southern Alps contain seventeen mountains which are over 3050m high. Central to the Mackenzie Country is lovely Lake Tekapo, which is 'guarded' by the stone Church of the Good Shepherd and a statue of a sheepdog.

MAIN ATTRACTIONS

- The **views** of Aoraki/Mount Cook from the Hermitage Hotel, Mount Cook village.
- **Skiing** on the **Tasman Glacier**, New Zealand's largest.
- The **views** of **Lake Tekapo** and the **Church of the Good Shepherd**.
- A **helicopter ride** over Aoraki/Mount Cook and the Tasman glacier.
- A visit to a **salmon farm**.
- Watching the **kaki/black stilt** — the world's rarest wading bird.
- Driving through the picturesque Lindis Pass.
- **Walking** the Hooker Valley Track (3—4 hours return).

Right: *The Church of the Good Shepherd, Lake Tekapo, built in 1935 to commemorate the region's pioneers.*

USEFUL CONTACTS

Information Centres:
Fairlie
The Heartlands Fairlie Resource &
Information Centre,
64 Main Street, Fairlie,
tel: (03) 685 8496, fax: (03) 685 8449,
e-mail: fairlie@xtra.co.nz
website: www.fairlie.co.nz
Lake Tekapo
Kiwi Treasures, Gifts & Information,
SH8, Lake Tekapo,
tel/fax: (03) 680 6686,
Lake Pukaki
Lake Pukaki Visitor Centre,
SH8, Lake Pukaki,
tel: (03) 435 3280, fax: (03) 435 2383,
e-mail: lake.pukaki@xtra.co.nz
Aoraki/Mount Cook
Aoraki/Mount Cook National Park
Department of Conservation Visitor
Centre, Aoraki/Mount Cook,
tel: (03) 435 1186, fax: (03) 435 1080,
e-mail: mtcookvc@doc.govt.nz

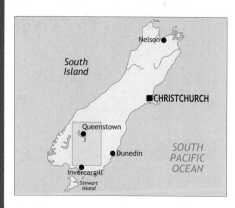

Queenstown and Central Otago

Queenstown and its surrounding region together comprise New Zealand's premier adventure playground. No other region in the country has so many beautiful natural attractions, and none has an infrastructure as well developed as Queenstown's, to maximize visitors' enjoyment of the district's outdoor pursuits. With its lakeside setting, overlooked by spectacular mountains, Queenstown enjoys a sublime location. All year round this region draws visitors from overseas and other parts of New Zealand, who relish its lake, canyon and mountain splendour. The Queenstown region has also become very popular as a location for film-makers from overseas.

MAIN ATTRACTIONS

- **Jet-boating** on the Dart River or in Skippers Canyon, Shotover River.
- A cruise on Lake Wakatipu to **Walter Peak High Country Farm.**
- A trip on the **Skyline Gondola** up to the **Skyline Restaurant.**
- **Driving** over the **Crown Range** to Cardrona and Wanaka.
- Taking a **'Lord of the Rings' tour** of the film trilogy's locations.
- **Bungee jumping** in the area where it was pioneered.
- Tramping in **Mount Aspiring National Park.**
- Visiting to the **Warbirds Museum.**
- **Sample wine** in the **Kawarau Gorge wineries.**
- Walking in **Queenstown Gardens.**
- Visiting the **Lakes District Museum** in Arrowtown.

Right: Jet-boating in Skippers Canyon on the Shotover River, north of Queenstown, is one of the many adventure activities available.

USEFUL CONTACTS

Queenstown i-SITE Visitor Centre: Clocktower Centre, cnr Shotover and Camp Streets, Queenstown, tel: (03) 442 4100, fax: (03) 442 8907, freephone: 0800 668 888, e-mail: info@qvc.co.nz website: www.queenstown-vacation.com
Destination Queenstown: 44 Stanley Street, Queenstown, freephone: 0800 478 336, tel: (03) 441 0700, fax: (03) 442 7441, e-mail: queenstown@xtra.co.nz website: www.queenstown.co.nz
Lake Wanaka Visitor Information Centre: 100 Ardmore Street, Lakefront, Wanaka, tel: (03) 443 1233, fax: (03) 443 1290, e-mail: wanakainfo@yahoo.com.au website: www.lakewanaka.co.nz

A   76   B   C   73   D

1

2

81

3

4

5

77

94

96

Lake Unknown
Mt Aspiring National Park
Lake Neriae
Humboldt Mtns
Mt Earnslaw 2816 m
Centaur Peaks 2525 m
Mt Ferguson 2484 m
End Peak 2100 m
Maungawera Albert Town
Hawea Flat
Georges Hill 891 m
Paradise
Stair Peak 2175 m
Glendhu Bay
Wanaka
Skyshow Centre
Lindis Valley
Cambrians
Mt Alfred 1375 m
Mt Aurum 2245 m
Mt Barker
Luggate
8A
8
Cluden
Ailsa Mtns
Kinloch
Glenorchy
1733 m
Skippers Canyon
Queensberry
Tarras
Drybread
Becks
Pigeon Island
Home Hill 1608 m
Major Peak 2126 m
Mt Gilbert 1783 m
Coronet Peak 1651 m
Arrowtown
Cardrona
Mt Pisa
Bendigo
Crippletown
Dunstan Mountains
Matakanui
Lauder
Elfin Bay
Pig Island
Mt Creighton
Wharehuanui
Lower Shotover
Crown Terrace
Mt Allen 1492 m
Lowburn
Lowburn
8
Dunstan 1667 m
Omakau
Ophir
Round Peaks 1763 m 1759 m
Skyline Gondola
Queenstown
Fernhill
Arrow Junction
Kawarau Bridge
Gibbston
6
Ripponvale
Cromwell
Chatto Creek
85
Poolburn
Mt Nicholas
Kelvin Heights
Frankton
Bannockburn
8
Clyde Dam
Clyde
Muttontown
Moa Creek
Galloway
Mt Mavora 1990 m
Lake Wakatipu
Mt Salmond 1640 m
Nevis Crossing
Earnscleugh
Alexandra
Walter Peak
Cecil Peak 1974 m
Collins Bay
The Remarkables
Mt Black 1604 m
Lower Nevis
Conroys Gully
Butchers Gully
Little Valley
Roxburgh Reservoir
Wither Peak 1773 m
Ridge Peak 1841 m
Flag 1692 m
Fruitlands
8
Lake Roxburgh
Manorburn Reservoir
North Mavora Lake
Hector Mtns
Rocky Mount 1889 m
Gorge Creek
Coal
Greenland Reservoir
Jane Peak 2022 m
Eyre Peak 1968 m
Kingston Flyer
Shingle Creek
Lake Onslow
Bald Hill 1395 m
Kingston
Tennants Peak 1502 m
Titan Rocks 1253 m
Coal Creek Flat
Roxburgh Hydro
West Dome 1269 m
6
Fairlight
Garston
Nokomai
Blue Lake
Blue
Umbrella Mtns
Roxburgh
Rocky Hill 567 m
Mossburn
Athol
Garvie Mtns
Dumbarton
Teviot
Castlerock
Parawa
East Dome 1350 m
Flat Hill 776 m
Ettrick
Millers Flat
Five Rivers
Lowther
Cattle Flat
Waikaia
Craig Flat
Lumsden
Dunrobin
Island Block
Lintley
Longridge North
Mount Wendon 845 m
Park Hill
Edievale
Raes Junction
Beaumont
Josephville
St Patricks
Waiparu
90
Heriot
Crookston
Craigellachie
Gabriels Gully
Bowlers Creek
Caroline
Balfour
94
Waipounamu
Wendon
Greenvale
Crossans Corner
Kelso
Black Gully
Tuapeka West
Evans Flat
Dipton West
Glenure
Riversdale
Pyramid
Waikaka
Merino Downs
Glenkenich
Tapanui
Pomahaka
Rongahere
Kononi
Lawrence
Tuapeka Flat
Dipton
637 m
Ben More
Waimea Hill 671 m
Mandeville
Otama
Chatton
Maitland
Waikaka Valley
Waikoikoi
Rankleburn
Waitahuna West
Tuapeka Mouth
Opio
Wreys Bush
Pukemutu
Dunearn
Croydon
Whiterigg
Willowbank
90
Benio
Conical Hill
Waipahi
Wharetoa
Greenfield
Puketi
Heddon Bush
Centre Bush
Limehills
Otapiri
West Peak 587 m
Hokonui
Gore
East Gore
Pukerau
1
Arthurton
Kaiwera
Wairuna
Popotunoa
Clydevale
Awamangu
Bayswater
Oreti Plains
Lady Barkly
Winton
Browns
Waimumu
Tuamata
Ashley Downs
Clifton
Pukeawa
Pukepito
Gladfield
Drummond

79

75

Fiordland

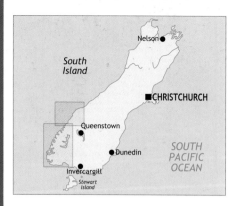

Fiordland is New Zealand's most remote but dramatically beautiful region. A place of primeval purity, most of the region is a national park, and some parts have been designated as a World Heritage Area. Fiordland is a region of towering sounds, tumbling cataracts, glacial lakes and virgin forests. It has only one town, Te Anau, which makes an ideal base for an exploration of the lakes Te Anau and Manapouri and Milford Sound. Overlooked by Mitre Peak (1692m), Milford Sound is a place of breathtaking beauty, while the area around Te Anau abounds in great walking tracks such as the Milford and the Kepler.

MAIN ATTRACTIONS

- Taking a day or overnight cruise on **Milford Sound**.
- Sleeping on board an overnight cruise to Doubtful Sound.
- Walking one of **Te Anau**'s many fine tracks.
- Visiting the **West Arm Underground Power Station** at Lake Manapouri.
- Observing **dolphins**, **seals** and **penguins** while cruising on the fiords.
- Taking a **helicopter** ride over the sounds and surrounding mountains.

Above: The shore of Milford Sound, Fiordland, overlooked by Mitre Peak in the centre.

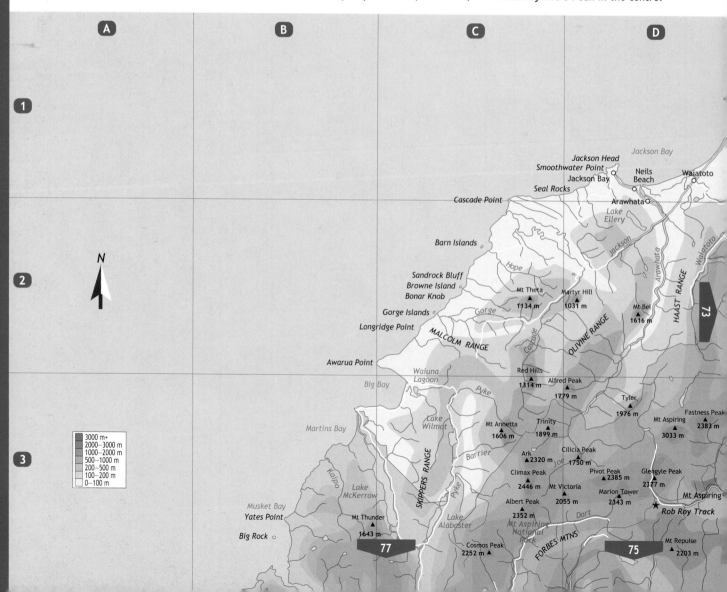

A

B

C

D

1

2

75

3

4

5

3000 m+
2000–3000 m
1000–2000 m
500–1000 m
200–500 m
100–200 m
0–100 m

N

Milford Sound
Mitre Peak
1692 m
Milford Track
The Chasm
Access Peak
1865 m
Mt Talbot
2105 m
Hollyford
Lake Marian
Lake Adelaide
Lake Ada
Lake Moreton
Bell Point
Sutherland Sound
Rugged Mtn
1166 m
Tommy Point
Bligh Sound
Flat Point
Bounty Haven
Mt Longsight
1482 m
Lake Grave
Lake Dark
Fiordland National Park
Barrier Peak
1966 m
Mt Anau
1958 m
Lake Thompson
Lake Erskine
Lake Gunn
Cascade Creek
George Sound
Rugged Peak
1206 m
FRANKLIN MTNS
Worsley
Clinton
Arthur
Castle
EARL MTNS
Eglinton
94
Knobs Flat
Round Head
Looking Glass Bay
Two Thumb Bay
Mt Elder
1197 m
George
Lake Alice
Mt McDougall
2036 m
North Fiord
LIVINGSTONE MTNS
Mt Tanilba
1242 m
Expedition Peak
1314 m
Mt Elwood
1256 m
Lake Hankinson
End Peak
1250 m
Mirror Lakes
Acheron Lakes
Caswell Sound
Nugget Point
Islet Point
Charles Sound
Hawes Head
Mt Paulina
1140 m
Lake Marchant
Irene
Lake Wapiti
Lake Mackinnon
Lake Bloxham
Middle Fiord
Lake Te Anau
Te Anau Downs
94
Mt Richmond
1674 m
Nancy Sound
Anxiety Point
Thompson Sound
Colonial Head
Mt Napier
1195 m
Double Peak
1484 m
Lake Duncan
Hidden Lake
Lake Te Au
MURCHISON MTNS
Dana Peak
1722 m
Camelot
Ettrick Burn
Point Burn
Te Anau Hill
504 m
Bare Peak
1208 m
South West Point
Nee Islets
Secretary Island
Doubtful Sound
Shelter Island
Febrero Point
Bauza Island
Mt Forbes
1305 m
Medley Peak
1231 m
Lake Dora
Lake Minerva
Mt Maury
1570 m
South Fiord
Lake Herries
Dagg Sound
Towing Head
Lake Paradise
Depth Peak
1161 m
Calm Peak
1109 m
Lake Swan
Hall Arm
Matapsina Reach
Mt George
1598 m
Norwest Lake
Iris Burn
Woro
Te Anau
Wildlife Centre
Lake Manapouri
Lake Thomas
Awe Burn
95
Lake Beattie
Vancouver Arm
Mt Troup
1518 m
Fiordland National Park
Broughton Arm
Mt Grey
1506 m
Lake Lois
94
Manapouri
Mararoa
The Key
Breaksea Island
Gilbert Islands
Harbour Islands
Mt Watson
1518 m
Mt Cusack
1612 m
Cone Peak
1509 m
Paddock Hill
899 m
Lake Rakatu
North Braxtan
1080 m
Gladstone Peak
1569 m
Mt Wales
972 m
Oke Island
Mt Forster
1137 m
Wet Jacket Arm
Acheron Passage
Mt Reeves
1183 m
Loch Maree
HUNTER MTNS
Whare
Aparima
White Hill
1398 m
Redcliff
TAKITIMU MTNS
Telford Burn
Resolution Island
Mt Lyall
994 m
Parrot Island
Porpoise Point
Long Island
Cooper Island
HEATH MTNS
Long Burn
Orauea
Lake Hay
MERRIE RANGE
Mt Puteketeke
1558 m
Island Lake
Borland Burn
Waiau
Monowai
Etal
932 m
Anchor Island
Indian Island
Seal Islands
Cook Channel
Mt Edgecumbe
1204 m
Lake Mike
Sphinx Lake
Green Lake
Blackmount
Mt Bradshaw
981 m
Lake Cadman
Lake Widgeon
Lake Kakapo
White Peak
1539 m
Dean Hill
779 m
Ohai
Birchwood
Nightcaps
Wairio
Woodlaw
Lake Fraser
Lake Rimmer
Edwardson Sound
Lake Victor
Princess Burn
PRINCESS MTNS
Lake Monowai
KAHEREKOAU MTNS
Litt Burn
Otahu Flat
Eastern Bush
Feldwick
Scotts Gap
Aparima
Great Island
Harbour Island
1049 m
Cunaris Sound
Houseroof Hill
1349 m
CAMERON MTNS
Tower Peak
1405 m
Caroline Burn
Mary Island
Helmet Hill
606 m
Lake Hauroko
Waiau
Clifden
Orawia
Merrivale
Waikouro
Treble Mountain
Helena Peak
1387 m
Raymonds Gap
Providence Rocks
Chalky Island
Passage Island
Cording Island
Weka Island
Coal Island
Lake Monk
Lake Poteriteri
Lake Kiwi
Big
Lake Hakapoua
Crombie
Te Waewae Bay
Tuatapere
Pikopiko
Happy Valley
Otautau
Ringway
Papatotara
Te Tua
Waiau
Te Waewae
Fairfax
Puysegur Point
Preservation Inlet
Eastern Passage
Five Fingers Peninsula

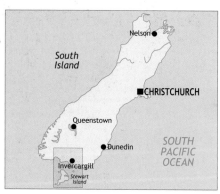

Southland and Stewart Island

Southland is New Zealand's southernmost province. Across Foveaux Strait from Southland's port, Bluff, is Stewart Island, the country's third largest island, also known as Rakiura. Southland has a great diversity of landscapes, from fertile rolling farmlands to pristine rainforests and long stretches of sandy coastline. Invercargill (57,000) is the capital of Southland and New Zealand's most southerly city. There are many fine walking tracks throughout Southland, such as the Hump Ridge Track, west of Tuatapere. The Catlins Forest Park, in the southeastern corner of Southland, is considered one of New Zealand's finest wilderness areas.

MAIN ATTRACTIONS

- The unspoiled forests and coastline of the **Catlins Forest Park**.
- **The Eastern Southland Art Gallery** and the **Fishing Museum** in Gore.
- **Ulva Island**, near Stewart Island, an open **bird sanctuary**.
- The walk out to the **lighthouse** at **Nugget Point**, Tokata, in the north of the Catlins (*see* map p. 81).
- Jurassic fossilized forest remains at low tide at Curio Bay.
- A day trip to **Oban**, the only settlement on Stewart Island.
- Sampling **Foveaux Strait's** gift to the gourmet world — Bluff oysters.
- Tramping the Hump Ridge Track.
- A ride on the 'Kingston Flyer', a **vintage train** going from Fairlight to Kingston.

Left: The view from Stewart Island towards neighbouring Iona Island.

TRAVEL TIPS

Websites:
www.events.southlandnz.com
www.myplace.southlandnz.com
Invercargill i-SITE Visitor Centre:
Southland Museum and Art Gallery,
Gala Street, Invercargill,
tel: (03) 214 6243, fax: (03) 218 4415,
e-mail: invercargill.
i-site@venturesouthland.co.nz
website: www.invercargill.org.nz
Gore i-SITE Visitor Centre: cnr
Norfolk St & Hokonui Drive, Gore,
tel: (03) 203 9288, fax: (03) 203 9286,
e-mail: goreinfo@goredc.govt.nz
website: www.gorenz.com
Bluff Visitor Terminal:
21 Foreshore Road, Bluff,
freephone: 0800 000 511,
tel: (03) 212 7600, fax: (03) 212 8377,
e-mail: info@sie.co.nz website:
www.stewartislandexperience.co.nz

Dean Hill
79 m

A   77   B   C   75   D

Pyramid
Waikaka
Merino
Downs

Dipton
Otama
Chatton
Maitland
Waikakoi

637 m
Ben More
Mandeville
Knapdale
Waikaka
Valley

HOKONUI HILLS
Waimea Hill
Croydon
94
Willowbank

Ohai
Opio
671 m
Otamita
Otamita
90
Bemio

Birchwood
Nightcaps
6
Whiterigg
Otikerama

Eastern
Bush
Wairio
Wreys
Bush
Pukemutu
Pukearuhe
Otapiri
West Peak
587 m
Durndale
Waimumu
Gore
East
Gore
Pukerau
1

Otahu Flat
Feldwick
Woodlaw
Dunearn
Centre Bush
Limehills
Hokonui
Charlton
Kaiwera
1

Clifden
Orawia
Scotts Gap
Aparima
Heddon
Bush
96
Lady Barkly
Waimumu
Charlton
Ferndale
Otaraia

Merrivale
Waikouro
Bayswater
Gladfield
Otapiri
Te Tipua
1
Mataura
Waikana

Raymonds
Gap
Otautau
Ringway
Oreti
Plains
Winton
Browns
96
Waitane
Brydone
Tuturau
Waiarikiki

Pikopiko
Happy
Valley
Fairfax
Drummond
Thomsons
Crossing
Springhills
Hedgehope
Ota Creek
Wyndham
Oware

Tuatapere
Te Tua
Ermedale
Isla
Bank
Northope
Wilsons
Crossing
Lochiel
Tussock
Creek
Mabel
Bush
98
Dacre
Edendale
Menzies
Ferry
Redan
Mt Herbert
484 m

Papatotara
Te Waewae
Waihoaka
Gummies
Bush
Thornbury
Spar Bush
Ryal Bush
Grove
Bush
Rakahouka
1
Morton
Mains
Seaward
Downs
Glenham
Mokoreta

99
Gropers
Bush
Hazletts
Wrights
Bush
Branxholme
Roslyn
Bush
Woodlands
Longbush
Oteramika
Mataura
Island

Orepuki
Pahia Hill
227 m
Waipango
Waimatuku
6
Makarewa
Myross
Bush
Kennington
Rimu
Waituna
Mokotua
Gorge
Road
Pine Bush
Fortification

Pahia Point
Pahia
Colac
Bay
Longwood
99
Otaitai
Bush
Wallacetown
Lorneville
Roslyn
Bush
Kapuka
South
Ashers
Titiroa
Te Peka

Ruahine
Wakaputu
Riverton
The Rocks
West
Plains
Invercargill
Tisbury
Waimatua
Timpanys
Waimahaka

Old Man Rock
Oraka Point
Howells Point
Otatara
New
River
Estuary
Woodend
Motu Rimu
Oteramika
Kapuka
South
Tokanui
Quarry
Hills

Wakaputa Point
Pig Island
Oreti Beach
Awarua
Awarua
Wetlands
Waituna
Lagoon
Fortrose
Haldane

Centre
Island
Escape Reefs
Bombay Rock
Steep Head
Greenhills
1
Awarua Bay
Otara
Slope
Point
Fossil
Forest

Hapuka Rock
Barracouta Point
Greenpoint
Bluff
Harbour
Toetoes Bay
Waipapa Point
Slope Point
Haldane
Bay
Curio
Bay

Shag Rock
Ocean Beach
Bluff
Tiwai Point
3

Lookout Point
Dog Island

Bishops and Clerks
Islands
North Head

Cave Point
Black Rock Point
Ruapuke Island
Seal Rocks

Rugged Islands
Lucky Point
Saddle Point
Mt Anglem
Christmas Village
Bay
Bird Island
Green Island
Breaksea Island

The Knobbies
Roger Head
750 m
980 m
Garden Point
South Islets
South Point

Codfish Island
The Paps
610 m
Gull Rock Point
Edwards Island
(Motunui)
North Island
Womens Island
Hazelburgh
Group

Richards Point
THOMSON RIDGE
Bobs Point
Muttonbird Islands
Bunker Islets

Masons Head
Oban
(Halfmoon
Bay)
Ackers Point
Bench Island

Mason Bay
Paterson Inlet
Ulva
Island
Cow
Island
Carter Passage

Mt Rakeahua
681 m
Chew Tobacco Point
4

Ernest Islands
Big Glory
Bay
East Cape
Stewart
Island

Adams Hill
401 m
Stewart Island/
Rakiura
National Park
266 m
Adventure Hill
Pikaroro Bay
Weka Island

Doughboy Bay
Mt Allen
750 m
Shelter Point
Breaksea Islands

South Red
Head Point
DECEIT PEAKS
Tutaepawhati
Bay
Owen Island

Little Moggy
Island
North
Arm

Big Moggy
Island
Muttonbird
Islands
Putauhina
Island
Cook Arm
Pearl Island
Port Pegasus
Seal Point
Black Rock

Big South
Cape Island
470 m
South
Arm
Noble Island
Ernest Island

South West
Cape
Murphy
Island
South Cape
Broad Head
Kaninihi Point

North Trap

3000 m+
2000–3000 m
1000–2000 m
500–1000 m
200–500 m
100–200 m
0–100 m

5

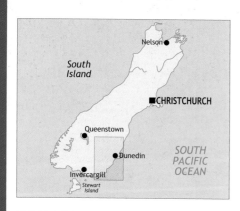

Dunedin and Coastal Otago

Dunedin reflects the character of its sturdy Scottish founders, its Victorian stone architecture being among the most striking in New Zealand. A stylish, compact city which is a pleasure to explore on foot, Dunedin is steeped in 19th-century history yet has kept up with the times, being a leading educational centre and home to some of New Zealand's most innovative fashion houses. No part of Dunedin is far from the sea. Out on the Otago Peninsula, just a 20-minute drive from the city centre, are wilderness areas which are habitats for unique native fauna, including the endangered Yellow-eyed Penguin, or Hoiho, and the magnificent Northern Royal Albatross.

MAIN ATTRACTIONS

- The ocean beaches of **St Clair, St Kilda** and **Tomahawk.**
- Cruising on **Otago Harbour**, to observe the **bird and marine life.**
- **Kayaking** on **Otago Harbour.**
- Visiting the **Oamaru Blue Penguin Colony**, a conservation area for the smallest penguins in the world.
- A **self-guided walk** in Oamaru's main street, to see its heritage buildings.
- A visit to **Tautuku Bay**, where the Catlins Forest almost borders the sea.
- Head to the dramatic **Nugget Point** and check out the **lighthouse.**
- A visit to the **Otago Coast Forest** south of Dunedin.

Above: *The Yellow-eyed Penguin, or Hoiho, the world's rarest penguin, emerges from its shelter on the Otago Peninsula.*
Left: *The Octagon, in the very centre of Dunedin, is overlooked by a statue of Scottish poet Robbie Burns and there is a writers' walk around the Octagon.*

USEFUL CONTACTS

The Dunedin Visitor Centre:
48 The Octagon, Dunedin,
tel: (03) 474 3300, fax (03) 474 3311,
e-mail: visitor.centre@dcc.govt.nz
website: www.dunedinNZ.com
Oamaru i-SITE Visitor Centre:
1 Thames Street, Oamaru,
tel: (03) 434 1656, fax: (03) 434 1657,
e-mail: info@tourismwaitaki.co.nz
Website: www.tourismwaitaki.co.nz

For **accommodation and dining** information: www.CityofDunedin.com
Dunedin Airport is located 30km south of the city.
Drive time from Dunedin to Oamaru is 1.5 hours, to Christchurch 3 hours.

A

85 Ophir
Chatto Creek
8
Clyde
Clyde Dam
Muttontown
Earnscleugh
Galloway
Alexandra
Conroys Gully
Little Valley
Butchers Gully
75
Fruitlands
8
Gorge Creek
Shingle Creek
Coal Creek Flat
Roxburgh Hydro
Roxburgh
Dumbarton
Teviot
Ettrick
Millers Flat
8
Craig Flat
Island Block
Raes Junction
Dunrobin
90
Edievale
Park Hill
Heriot
Crookston
Kelso
Black Gully
Tapanui
Glenkenich
Rongahere
Pomahaka
Rankleburn
Comical Hill
Waipahi
Popotunoa
Tuamata
Clydevale
Wairuna
Ashley Downs
Clifton
Clinton
Waiwera South
Kuriwao
79
Mt Rosebery
719 m
Purekireki
Lochindorb
Awatea
Ajax Hill
700 m
Owaka Valley
Tawanui
Houipapa
Tahakopa
Caberfeidh
Black Horn
363 m
Maclennan
Papatowai
Chaslands
MACLENNAN RANGE

B

Poolburn
Moa Creek
NORTH ROUGH RIDGE
Maori
Manorburn Reservoir
Roxburgh
Reservoir
ROUGH RIDGE
Manorburn Reservoir
Linn Burn
Greenland Reservoir
Lake Onslow
Rocky Hill 567 m
Spillers Hill
Shepard's Hut
960 m
Teviot
LAMMERLAW RANGE
Tuapeka West
Evans Flat
Lawrence
Tuapeka Flat
Waitahuna
Waitahuna West
8
Round Hill
Craigellachie
Bowlers Creek
Gabriels Gully
Beaumont
Tuapeka Mouth
Puketi
Manuka Creek
Wharetoa
Greenfield
Awamangu
Hillend
Pukepito
Crichton
Pukeawa
Stony Creek
Mount Stuart
Adams Flat
Glenore
Milton
Tokoiti
Moneymore
Lovells Flat
1
Benhar
Te Houka
Warepa
Toiro
Waitepeka
Finegand
Otanomomo
Balclutha
Stirling
Kaitangata
Paretai
Romahapa
Port Molyneux
Glenomaru
Kaka Point
Campbell Point
Hays Gap
Owaka
Otekura
Kaimataitai
Pounawea
Nugget Point
Hinahina
Ratanui
Hayward Point
Tuhawaiki Island
White Head
Purakaunui
Tarara
Purakauiti
Cosgrove Island
Long Point
Catlins Forest Park
Cathedral Caves
Tautuku Bay
Tautuku Peninsula
The Sisters
Chaslands Mistake

C

Ranfurly
Gimmerburn
Kyeburn
85
Waipiata
Kokonga
Orangapai
87
Hamilton
Tiroiti
Patearoa
Hyde
Paerau
87
Ngapuna
Middlemarch
ROCK AND PILLAR RANGE
Rock and Pillar
Bald Hill 476 m
Sutton
Matarae
Mt Stoker
Shannon
Pukerangi
Taieri
Sutton
Clarks Junction
Hindon
Mt Allan
Lee Flat
Lee Stream
87
Harveys Flat
Woodside
Berwick
Wyllies Crossing
Mosgiel
Fairfield
Allanton
Scroggs Hill
Otokia
Henley
Ocean View
Brighton
1
Waihola
Clarendon
Kapiti
Milburn
Taieri Mouth
Helensbrook
Brooklands
Glenledi
Akatore
Quoin Point
Chrystalls Beach
Toko Mouth
Wangaloa
Coal Point
Summer Hill
Molyneux Bay
Taieri Island
Taieri Beach

D

71
Mt Dasher 1304 m
Reidston
Teschemakers
Maheno
Waimotu
Kakanui
Herbert
Waianakarua
Green Valley
679 m
Hampden
Moeraki Boulders
Moeraki
Hillgrove
Katiki
85
Shag Valley
Macraes Flat
Dunback
Inch Valley
Moonlight
Stoneburn
Glenpark
Meadowbank
Bushey
Shag Point
Palmerston
1
Yellow-Eyed Penguins
Nenthorn
Wairunga
Flag Swamp
Goodwood
Bobbys Head
Mt Royal 710 m
Hawkesbury Bush
Tumai
Waikouaiti
2
Merton
Cornish Head
Karitane
Puketeraki
Seacliff
Brinns Point
Evansdale
Warrington
Potato Point
HORSE RANGE
Shag
Taieri
Hindon
Upper Waitati
Waitati
Heywood Point
Aramoana
Taiaroa Head
Wharf Flat
Mihiwaka
1
Royal Albatross Colony
Port Chalmers
Otakou
Harwood
88
Glenleith
Broad Bay
Portobello
DUNEDIN
Pukehiki
Hoopers Inlet
Highcliff
Larnach Castle
Green Island
Maori Head
Cape Saunders
Black Head
Harakehe Head
3
Otago Peninsula
Otago Harbour

N

3000 m+
2000–3000 m
1000–2000 m
500–1000 m
200–500 m
100–200 m
0–100 m

TOURIST AREA AND TEXT INDEX

Note: numbers in **bold** denote photographs

MAIN MAP INDEX

Hastwell	55	B3
Hatepe	45	D4
Hatfield	68	C3
Hatuma	52	D3
Hauiti	49	B3
Haukawakawa	61	B2
Haumoana	53	B2
Haunui	55	C2
Haupiri	65	B3
Hauturu	45	A2
Hauwai	61	C5
Havelock North	53	B2
Havelock	61	B3
Hawai	47	D2
Hawarden	65	D4
Hawea Flat	73	B4
Hawera	51	B4
Hawk Hills	67	B3
Hawkens Junction	47	B2
Hawkesbury Bush	81	D2
Hawkswood	67	B4
Hays Gap	81	B5
Hazletts	79	B2
Heatherlea	55	A2
Hector	59	A4
Heddon Bush	75	A5
Hedgehope	79	C2
Helena Bay	39	B4
Helensbrook	81	B4
Helensville	41	C2
Henley	81	C3
Herbert	81	D1
Herbertville	55	D2
Herekino	37	C3
Herepo	63	B4
Heriot	75	C4
Hexton	49	B4
Hicks Bay	49	C1
Highbank	68	C2
Highcliff	81	D3
Hihi	37	C2
Hihitahi	52	B2
Hikuai	43	B4
Hikumutu	45	B4
Hikurangi	39	B4
Hikutaia	43	B4
Hikuwai	49	B3
Hilderthorpe	71	C5
Hillend	81	B4
Hillersden	61	A4
Hillgrove	81	D1
Hillsborough	51	B2
Himatangi Beach	55	A1
Himatangi	55	A2
Hinahina	81	B5
Hinakura	55	B4
Hinau	52	B3
Hindon	81	C3
Hinds	68	B4
Hinehopu	47	B2
Hinuera	45	C1
Hira	61	A3
Hiruharama	49	B2
Hiwinui	55	B1
Hodderville	45	C2
Hoe-O-Tainui	43	B5
Hohonu	63	D3
Hokio Beach	55	A2
Hokitika	63	C3
Hokonui	75	B5
Hollyford	77	D1
Homebush	69	A2
Homewood	55	C4
Honeymoon Valley	37	C3
Honikiwi	45	B2
Hoopers Inlet	81	D3
Hope	59	D3
Hopelands	55	C1
Hopeone	47	C3
Hopuhopu	43	A5
Hopuruahine Landing	47	C4
Horahia	43	B4
Horahora	39	B4
Horeke	37	D3
Hornby	69	C2
Horoera	49	C1
Horohoro	47	A2
Horokino	45	C3
Horomanga	47	B3
Horopito	52	A1
Hororata	68	C2
Horrellville	69	B1
Horsley Downs	65	D4
Hospital Hill	47	D2
Hot Water Beach	43	C3
Hoteo North	41	C1
Houhora Heads	37	B2
Houhora	37	B2
Houipapa	81	A5
Houpoto	49	A2
Houto	39	A5
Howard Junction	59	C4
Howard	59	C5
Howick	41	D3
Huanui	49	B3
Huapai	41	C3
Huarau	41	B1
Huia	41	C3
Huiarua	49	B2
Huinga	51	C3
Huiroa	51	C3
Hukanui	55	B2
Hukapapa	45	B5
Hukarere	65	B2
Hukatere	37	B2
Hukerenui	39	A4
Humphreys	63	C3
Hundalee	67	C3
Hunter	71	C4
Hunterville	52	B3
Huntingdon	68	C4
Huntly	43	A5
Hunua	41	D4
Hupara	39	A3
Hurford	51	A2
Hurleyville	51	C4
Hurunui Mouth	67	B4
Hurunui	67	A4
Hyde	81	C1
Idaburn	71	A5
Ihakara	55	A2
Ihungia	49	B2
Ihuraua	55	B3
Ikamatua	65	B3
Ikawai	71	C5
Inangahua Junction	59	A5
Inangahua Landing	59	A5
Inangahua	59	A5
Inch Valley	81	D2
Inchbonnie	63	D3
Inglewood	51	B3
Invercargill	79	C2
Isla Bank	79	B2
Island Bay	57	B4
Island Block	81	A3
Ivydale	37	C3
Iwikau Village	45	C5
Iwitahi	47	A4
Jackson Bay	76	D1
Jacksons	63	D3
Jacobs River	73	B1
Jerusalem	51	D4
Johnsonville	57	B4
Josephville	75	A4
Judgeford	57	B4
Kaeo	37	D3
Kaharoa	47	A2
Kahika	47	C5
Kahoe	37	D3
Kahutara	55	A4
Kaiapoi	69	C2
Kaiata	63	C3
Kaiatea	39	B4
Kaiaua	43	A4
Kaihere	43	B5
Kaihinu	63	C3
Kaihu	37	D5
Kai-Iwi	51	D5
Kaikohe	37	D4
Kaikou	39	A4
Kaikoura	67	C3
Kaimamaku	39	B4
Kaimarama	43	B3
Kaimata	51	B3
Kaimataitai	81	B5
Kaimaumau	37	C2
Kaimiro	51	B3
Kaingaroa Forest	47	B3
Kaingaroa	37	C2
Kaipaki	45	B1
Kaipara Flats	41	C2
Kaiparoro	55	B2
Kaipikari	51	B2
Kairakau Beach	53	B3
Kairanga	55	B1
Kairangi	45	C1
Kairara	37	D5
Kairua	47	A1
Kaitaia	37	C3
Kaitangata	81	B4
Kaitaratahi	49	A4
Kaitawa	47	C4
Kaiteriteri	59	D1
Kaitieke	45	B5
Kaitoke	51	D5
Kaituna	55	B3
Kaiwaka	41	C1
Kaiwera	75	C5
Kaiwhaiki	51	D5
Kaka Point	81	B4
Kaka	59	C4
Kakahi	45	B4
Kakahu Bush	68	A4
Kakanui	81	D1
Kakapotahi	63	B4
Kakaramea	51	C4
Kakariki	49	C2
Kakatahi	52	A2
Kamaka	63	D2
Kamo	39	B4
Kanakanaia	49	B3
Kaniere	63	C3
Kaniwhaniwha	45	B1
Kanohi	41	C2
Kapenga	47	A2
Kapiro	37	D3
Kapiti	81	B3
Kaponga	51	B3
Kapowairua	37	B1
Kapuka South	79	C2
Kapuni	51	B3
Karaka	41	D4
Karakariki	45	B1
Karamea	59	A3
Karamu	45	B1
Karangahake	43	B5
Karangarua	73	C1
Karapiro	45	C1
Karatia	37	B1
Karekare	41	C3
Kareponia	37	C2
Karewarewa	52	B3
Karioi	52	A1
Karitane	81	D2
Karori	57	B4
Karoro	63	C3
Katikati	43	C5
Katiki	81	D1
Katui	37	D4
Kauaeranga	43	B4
Kauangaroa	52	A3
Kaukapakapa	41	C2
Kauri	39	B4
Kauroa	45	A1
Kauru Hill	71	B5
Kauwhata	55	B1
Kawa	43	B1
Kawakawa Bay	43	A3
Kawakawa	39	A3
Kawatiri	59	C4
Kawautahi	45	B4
Kawerau	47	B2
Kawerua	37	C4
Kawhia	45	A2
Kawiti	39	A4
Kekerengu	61	B5
Kelchers	71	B4
Kelso	75	C5
Kelvin Heights	75	B2
Kenana	37	D2
Kenepuru Head	61	C3
Kennedy Bay	43	B2
Kennington	79	C2
Kerepehi	43	B4
Kereru	52	D2
Kererutahi	47	C2
Kereta	43	B3
Keretu	47	D3
Kerikeri Inlet	39	A3
Kerikeri	39	A3
Kerrytown	71	C3
Kia Ora	71	C5
Kihikihi	45	B2
Kihitu Pa	47	D5
Kikiwa	59	C4
Kilgram	61	B5
Killinchy	69	B3
Kimbell	71	B2
Kimberley	69	B2
Kimbolton	52	B3
Kina	59	D3
Kingsdown	71	C3
Kingseat	41	D4
Kingston	75	B3
Kinleith	45	D2
Kinloch	45	D3
Kinohaku	45	A2
Kiokio	45	B2
Kirikau	45	B4
Kirikopuni	39	A5
Kirioke	37	D4
Kiritaki	55	C1
Kiritehere	45	A2
Kirwee	69	B2
Kiwitea	55	B1
Knapdale	75	C5
Knobs Flat	77	D2
Koeke Junction	52	B2
Kohatu	59	C4
Kohe	37	C3
Kohekohe	41	D4
Kohi	51	C4
Kohika	71	C4
Kohinui	55	C2
Kohukohu	37	C3
Kohumaru	37	C3
Kohuratahi	45	A5
Koitiata	51	D5
Kokako	47	C4
Kokatahi	63	C4
Kokiri	63	D3
Kokoamo	71	B5
Kokonga	81	C1
Komako	52	B3
Komakorau	43	A5
Komata North	43	B4
Komata	43	B4
Komokoriki	41	C2
Kongahu	59	A3
Konini	55	B2
Kononi	75	D5
Kopane	55	B1
Kopara	65	B3
Kopu	43	B4
Kopua	55	D1
Kopuaranga	55	B3
Kopuaroa	49	B2
Kopuawhara	49	A5
Kopuku	43	A4
Kopuriki	47	B3
Korakonui	45	C2
Koranga	47	D3
Koremoa	41	A1
Korere	59	C4
Koriniti	51	D4
Korito	51	B3
Koromatua	45	B1
Koromiko	61	B3
Korora	55	C2
Kotare	45	A4
Kotemaori	47	C5
Kotinga	59	C2
Kotuku	63	D3
Kourawhero	41	C2
Koutu	37	C4
Kowai Bush	68	C1
Kowhai	67	C3
Kowhatu	71	B4
Kowhitirangi	63	C4
Kuaotunu	43	B3
Kumara Junction	63	C3
Kumara	63	C3
Kumeroa	55	C1
Kumeu	41	C3
Kupe	51	B3
Kuratau Junction	45	D4
Kuratau	45	C4
Kuripapango	52	D1
Kuriwa	81	A4
Kurow	71	B4
Kutarere	47	C2
Kyeburn Diggings	71	A5
Kyeburn	81	C1
Kyle	69	A3
Ladbrooks	69	C2
Lady Barkly	75	A5
Lagmhor	68	C3
Laingholm	41	C3
Lake Alice	55	A1
Lake Coleridge	63	D5
Lake Ferry	55	A4
Lake Grassmere	61	C4
Lake Hawea	73	A4
Lake Moeraki	73	A2
Lake Ohau Lodge	73	C3
Lake Ohia	37	C2
Lake Okataina	47	A2
Lake Paringa	73	B2
Lake Rotoma	47	B2
Lake Tekapo	71	B2
Lake Waitaki	71	B4
Lakeside	69	B3
Langridge	61	A5
Lansdown	71	C4
Lansdowne	69	C2
Larrys Creek	59	A5
Lauder	75	D2
Lauriston	68	C3
Lawrence	75	D5
Le Bons Bay	69	D3
Leamington	67	B4
Lee Flat	81	B3
Lee Stream	81	C3
Lees Valley	65	C5
Leeston	69	B3
Leigh	41	D1
Leithfield Beach	67	A5
Leithfield	65	D5
Lepperton	51	B2
Levels Valley	71	C3
Levels	71	C3
Levin	55	A2
Lichfield	45	D2
Lilybank	71	B1
Limehills	75	A5
Limestone Downs	41	D5
Lincoln	69	B2
Linden	57	B4
Lindis Valley	73	B5
Linkwater	61	B3
Lintley	75	B4
Linton	55	B2
Linwood	69	C2
Lismore	68	B3
Little Akaloa	69	D3
Little Bay	43	B2
Little Rakaia	69	B3
Little River	69	C3
Little Valley	81	A1
Little Waihi	47	B1
Little Wanganui	59	A3
Livingstone	71	B5
Loburn North	65	D5
Loburn	69	C1
Loch Norrie	41	C2
Lochiel	79	C2
Lochindorb	81	A4
Longbeach	68	C4
Longburn	55	B2
Longbush	55	B4
Longford	59	B5
Longlands	53	A2
Longridge North	75	B4
Longwood	79	B2
Lorneville	79	C2
Lovells Flat	81	B4
Lowburn	75	C2
Lowcliffe	68	B4
Lower Hutt	57	B4
Lower Kaimai	45	D1
Lower Kawhatau	52	B2
Lower Moutere	59	C3
Lower Nevis	75	C3
Lower Selwyn Huts	69	B3
Lower Shotover	75	B2
Lowther	75	A4
Luggate	73	A5
Lumsden	75	A4
Lyalldale	71	C3
Lyell	59	A5
Lyndhurst	68	C3
Lynton Downs	67	C3
Lyttelton	69	C2
Maata	51	B3
Mabel Bush	79	C2
Maclennan	81	A5
Macraes Flat	81	C1
Maerewhenua	71	B5
Maewa	55	B1
Mahakirau	43	B3
Mahana	59	D3
Mahanga	49	A5
Maharakeke	52	D3
Maheno	81	D1
Mahia Beach	49	A5
Mahia	49	A5
Mahinepua	37	D2
Mahitahi	73	B1
Mahoe	51	B3
Mahoenui	45	A3
Mahora	49	C2
Mahurangi West	41	C2
Mahurangi	41	C2
Mahuta	37	D5
Maihiihi	45	B2
Maimai	65	B2
Maioro Sands	41	D4
Mairoa	45	A3
Maitahi	37	D5
Maitland	75	C5
Makahu	51	C3
Makaka	45	A1
Makakaho Junction	51	D4
Makakaho	51	D4
Makara Beach	57	B4
Makara	57	B4
Makarau	41	C2
Makaretu	52	C3
Makarewa	79	C2
Makarora	73	A3
Maketu	47	B1
Makino	55	B1
Makirikiri South	52	A3
Makomako	45	A1
Makorori	49	B4
Makotuku	55	C1
Makuri	55	C2
Mamaku	45	D2
Mamaranui	37	D5
Manaia	43	B3
Manakau	55	A2
Mananui	63	C3
Manapouri	77	C3
Manaroa	61	B3
Manawaru	43	B5
Mandeville North	69	C2
Mandeville	75	B5
Mangaeturoa	52	A1
Mangahei	55	D1
Mangaiti	43	B5
Mangakahu Valley	45	D4
Mangakino	45	C3
Mangakura	41	C2
Mangakuri Beach	53	B3
Mangamahu	52	A3
Mangamaire	55	B2
Mangamaunu	67	C3
Mangamingi	51	C3
Mangamuka Bridge	37	C3
Mangamuka	37	C3
Mangamutu	55	B2
Mangaonoho	52	B3
Mangaorapa	55	D1
Mangaore	55	A2
Mangaorongo	45	B2
Mangaotake	45	A3
Mangapa	37	D3
Mangapai	39	B5
Mangapakeha	55	C3
Mangaparo	45	A4
Mangapehi	45	B3
Mangapiko Valley	43	A5
Mangapiko	45	B1
Mangarakau	59	B1
Mangarawa	55	C1
Mangarimu	52	B3
Mangatainoka	55	C2
Mangataiore	37	C3
Mangatangi	43	A4
Mangatara	37	D5
Mangataraire	37	D3
Mangatarata	43	A4
Mangatawhiri	43	A4
Mangateparu	43	B5
Mangatoi	47	A1
Mangatoki	51	B3
Mangatoro	55	C1
Mangatu	37	D4
Mangatuna	49	B3
Mangawara	43	A5
Mangaweka	52	B3
Mangawhai	41	C1
Mangawhero	45	B2
Mangawhio	51	C4
Mangere	41	D3
Mangles Valley	59	B5
Mangonui	37	C2
Manoeka	47	A1
Manui	52	B2
Manuka Creek	81	B3
Manukau	37	C3
Manunui	45	B4
Manurewa	41	D3
Manutahi	51	B4
Manutuke	49	A4
Mapiu	45	B3
Mapua	59	D3
Mara	55	C2
Maraehara	49	C1
Maraekakaho	52	D2
Maraeroa	37	D3
Maraetaha	49	A4
Maraetai	41	D3
Marahau	59	D1
Maramarua	43	A4
Mararewa	59	C4
Maratoto	43	B4
Mariri	59	D3
Market Cross	59	A3
Marlow	39	A4

Marohemo	41	B1
Marokopa	45	A2
Maronan	68	B3
Maropiu	37	D5
Marsden Bay	39	B5
Marsden	63	C3
Marshland	69	C2
Marshlands	61	B4
Martinborough	55	A4
Marton Block	52	B3
Marton	52	A3
Maruia Springs	65	C3
Maruia	65	C2
Marumaru	47	D5
Marybank	59	D3
Massey University	55	B2
Masterton	55	B3
Mata	37	C3
Matahanea	47	D2
Matahapa	47	C2
Matahi	47	C3
Matahiwi	51	D4
Matahuru	43	A5
Matai	45	C1
Mataikona	55	C3
Matakana	41	C1
Matakanui	75	D2
Matakawau	41	D4
Matakitaki	59	B5
Matakohe	41	B1
Matamata	45	D1
Matamau	55	C1
Matangi	45	C1
Matangirau	37	D2
Matapihi	47	A1
Matapouri	39	B4
Matapu	51	B3
Matarae	81	C2
Matarangi	43	B3
Matarau	39	B4
Mataraua	37	D4
Matarawa	55	A3
Matariki	59	C4
Mataroa	52	B2
Matata	47	B2
Matatoki	43	B4
Matau	51	C3
Mataura Island	79	D2
Mataura	79	D2
Matauri Bay	37	D2
Matawai	47	D3
Matawaia	39	A4
Matawhero	49	B4
Matea	47	B4
Matiere	45	B4
Matihetihe	37	C4
Maungapohatu	47	C4
Maungatapere	39	B5
Maungatautari	45	C1
Maungati	71	C3
Maungatiro	71	B4
Maungatupoto	45	B3
Maungaturoto	41	C1
Maungawera	73	A4
Mauriceville West	55	B3
Mauriceville	55	B3
Mawaro	71	C3
Mawheraiti	65	B2
Maxwell	51	D5
Mayfield	68	B3
Maytown	71	C4
McLeans Island	69	B2
McLeod Bay	39	B5
Meadowbank	81	D2
Medbury	65	D4
Melling	57	B4
Menzies Ferry	79	D2
Mercer	41	D4
Meremere	41	D4
Meremere	51	B4
Meringa	45	D4
Merino Downs	75	C5
Merino Downs	79	D1
Merita	37	C2
Merrivale	77	D5
Merrivale	79	A1
Merton	81	D2
Mesopotamia	71	C1
Methven	68	C2
Middle Valley	71	C2
Middlehurst	61	A5
Middlemarch	81	C2
Midhurst	51	B3
Mihi	47	A3
Mihiwaka	81	D3
Mikimiki	55	B3
Miko	59	A4
Milburn	81	B4
Milford Sound	77	D1
Mill Creek	43	B3
Millers Flat	81	A2
Millerton	59	A4
Milltown	69	B3
Milnthorpe	59	C2
Milton	81	B4
Mina	67	B4
Minginui	47	B4
Miramar	57	B4
Miranda	43	A4
Mirza	61	B5
Mitcham	68	C3
Mitchells	63	D3
Mitimiti	37	C4
Moa Creek	75	D2
Millers Flat	75	D4
Moa Creek	81	B1
Moana	63	D3
Moawhango	52	B2
Moeatoa	45	A2
Moeawatea	51	C4
Moehau	37	D4
Moengawahine	39	A4
Moeraki	81	D1
Moerangi	45	A1
Moerewa	39	A4
Moeroa	51	C3
Mohaka	47	C5
Mohakatino	51	C1
Mohuiti	37	C3
Mokai	45	D3
Mokara	47	C5
Mokau	39	B4
Mokauiti	45	B3
Mokihinui	59	A4
Mokoia	51	B4
Mokoreta	79	D2
Mokotua	79	C2
Molesworth	67	B2
Monavale	45	C1
Moneymore	81	B4
Monowai	77	C4
Montalto	68	B3
Moonlight	81	C2
Morere	49	A5
Morrinsville	43	B5
Morrisons Bush	55	A4
Morrisons	81	C1
Morton Mains	79	C2
Morven	71	C4
Mosgiel	81	C3
Mossburn	75	A4
Motairehe	43	B1
Motakotako	45	A1
Motatau	39	A4
Motea	55	C1
Moteo	53	A2
Motu Rimu	79	C2
Motu	47	D3
Motueka	59	D3
Motukaika	71	C3
Motukarara	69	C3
Motukiore	37	D4
Motunau Beach	67	B5
Motunui	51	B2
Motuoapa	45	D4
Motupiko	59	C4
Motupipi	59	C2
Motutangi	37	B2
Motutere	45	D4
Motuti	37	C3
Motutoa	37	C4
Mount Bruce	55	B3
Mount Hutt	68	B2
Mount Maunganui	47	A1
Mount Possession	68	A3
Mount Stuart	81	B4
Mourea	47	A2
Moutoa	55	A2
Moutohora	47	D3
Mt Allan	81	C3
Mt Aspiring	76	D3
Mt Barker	73	A5
Mt Biggs	55	B1
Mt Creighton	75	A2
Mt Furneaux	67	C3
Mt Fyffe	67	C3
Mt Nessing	71	B3
Mt Nicholas	75	A2
Mt Peel	68	A3
Mt Pisa	73	B5
Mt Pleasant	61	B3
Mt Somers	68	B3
Mt Stoker	81	C2
Mt Wesley	37	D5
Muhunoa East	55	A2
Muhunoa	55	A2
Mukahanga	61	B2
Murchison	59	B5
Muriwai Beach	41	C3
Muriwai	49	A4
Murupara	47	B3
Muttontown	81	A1
Myross Bush	79	C2
Naike	41	D5
Napier	53	B2
Naseby	71	A5
National Park	45	B5
Neils Beach	76	D1
Nelson Creek	63	D2
Nelson	59	D3
Nenthorn	81	C2
Ness Valley	43	A3
Netherton	43	B4
Nevis Crossing	75	C2
New Brighton	69	C2
New Creek	59	A5
New Lynn	41	C3
New Plymouth	51	B2
Newall	51	A3
Newland	68	C3
Newman	55	B2
Newton Flat	59	A5
Ngaere	51	B3
Ngahape	45	B2
Ngahere	63	D2
Ngahinapouri	45	B1
Ngakawau	59	A4
Ngakonui	45	B4
Ngakuru	47	A3
Ngamatapouri	51	C4
Ngamoko	52	C3
Ngapaenga	45	A2
Ngapara	71	B5
Ngapuhi	37	D4
Ngapuke	45	D4
Ngapuna	47	A2
Ngaputahi	47	B4
Ngarimu Bay	43	B4
Ngaroma	45	C2
Ngaruawahia	43	A5
Ngataki	37	B2
Ngatamahine	45	B3
Ngatapa	49	A4
Ngatea	43	B4
Ngatimoti	59	C3
Ngatira	45	D2
Ngaturi	55	C2
Ngawaka	52	B2
Ngawapurua	55	C2
Ngawaro	47	A2
Ngawha Springs	37	D4
Ngawihi	55	A5
Ngongotaha	47	A2
Ngunguru	39	B4
Ngutunui	45	B2
Ngutuwera	51	C4
Nightcap	79	B1
Nightcaps	77	D5
Nihoniho	45	B4
Nikau	55	B2
Nireaha	55	B2
Nobles	65	B3
Nokomai	75	B3
Nopera	61	B3
Normanby	51	B4
Norsewood	52	C3
North Egmont	51	B3
North River	39	B5
Northope	79	B2
Norwood	69	B2
Notown	63	D2
Nuhaka	49	A5
Nukuhau	45	D3
Nukuhou North	47	C2
Nukumaru	51	C4
Nukutawhiti	37	D4
Oaklands	69	C2
Oakleigh	39	B5
Oakura	39	B4
Oamaru	71	C5
Oaonui	51	A3
Oaro	67	C3
Oban (Halfmoon Bay)	79	B4
Ocean Beach	39	B5
Ocean View	81	C3
Oeo	51	A4
Ohaaki	47	A3
Ohai	77	D4
Ohakea	55	A1
Ohakune	52	A1
Ohakuri	45	D3
Ohangai	51	B4
Ohau	55	A2
Ohaua	47	C3
Ohauiti	47	A1
Ohaupo	45	B1
Ohautira	45	A1
Ohineakai	49	C2
Ohinepaka	47	D5
Ohinepanea	47	B1
Ohinewai	43	A5
Ohingaiti	52	B3
Ohiwa	47	D2
Ohotu	52	B2
Ohui	43	C4
Ohura	45	A4
Ohuri	37	C4
Oio	45	B4
Okaeria	43	A4
Okahu	37	C3
Okahukura	45	B4
Okaiawa	51	B4
Okaihau	37	D3
Okains Bay	69	D3
Okapu	45	A1
Okaramio	61	B4
Okarito	63	A5
Okato	51	A3
Okau	51	C2
Okauia Pa	45	D1
Okauia	45	D1
Okere Falls	47	A2
Okete	45	A1
Okiato	39	A3
Okiore	47	D2
Okitu	49	B4
Okiwi Bay	61	A3
Okiwi	43	B1
Okoia	51	D5
Okoki	51	C2
Okoroire	45	D1
Okuku	65	D5
Okupu	43	B1
Okura	41	C2
Omaha	41	D1
Omahu	43	B4
Omakere	53	A3
Omamari	37	D5
Omana Beach	41	D3
Omana	39	A5
Omanawa Falls	45	D1
Omanawa	45	D1
Omapere	37	C4
Omarama	71	A4
Omarumutu	47	D2
Omata	51	A2
Omatane	52	B2
Omaunu	37	D3
Omiha	41	D3
Omihi	67	A5
Omoana	51	C3
Omokoroa Beach	43	C5
Omori	45	D4
Omoto	63	C3
Onaero	51	B2
One Tree Hill	41	D3
Onekaka	59	C2
Onemana	43	C4
Onepoto	47	C4
Onerahi	39	B5
Oneriri	41	C1
Oneroa	41	D3
Onetangi	43	A3
Onewhero	41	D4
Ongaonga	52	D3
Ongarue	45	B3
Ongaruru	49	C2
Onoke	37	C4
Opahi	39	A4
Opaki	55	B3
Opaku	51	C4
Opapa	53	A3
Opape	47	D2
Opara	37	C4
Oparara	59	A3
Oparau	45	A2
Oparure	45	B2
Opatu	45	B4
Ophir	81	A1
Opihi	68	A4
Opiki	55	A2
Opio	75	A5
Opito	43	C3
Oponae	47	D3
Opononi	37	C4
Opotiki	47	D2
Opouriao	47	C2
Opoutama	49	A5
Opouteke	37	D4
Opoutere	43	C4
Opua	39	A3
Opuatia	41	D5
Opuawhanga	39	B4
Opuha	68	A4
Opunake	51	A3
Oraka Beach	49	A5
Orakau	45	C2
Orakei Korako	45	D3
Orangapai	81	C1
Orangimea	51	D4
Oraora	37	C4
Orapiu	43	A3
Orari Bridge	68	B4
Orari	68	B4
Orautoha	45	B5
Orautoha	52	A1
Orawia	77	D5
Orepuki	79	A2
Orere Point	43	A3
Oreti Beach	79	B2
Oreti Plains	75	A5
Orewa	41	C2
Oringi	55	C1
Orini	43	A5
Ormond	49	A4
Oromahoe	39	A3
Orongo	43	B4
Orongorongo	57	B5
Oropi	47	A1
Oroua Downs	55	A1
Orton	41	D5
Orua Bay	41	C4
Oruaiti Beach	49	B1
Oruaiti	37	D2
Oruaiwi	45	D4
Oruanui	45	D3
Oruatua	45	D4
Oruawharo	41	C1
Oruru	37	C3
Ostend	41	D3
Ota Creek	79	C2
Otaha	39	A3
Otahu Flat	77	D5
Otahuti	79	B2
Otaika	39	B5
Otaio Gorge	71	C3
Otaio	71	C4
Otairi	52	A3
Otaitai Bush	79	B2
Otakairangi	39	A4
Otakeho	51	A4
Otaki Beach	57	C3
Otaki Forks	55	A3
Otaki	55	A3
Otakiri	47	B2
Otakou	81	D3
Otama	75	C5
Otamakapua	52	B3
Otamarakau	47	B1
Otamaroa	49	B1
Otamauri	52	D2
Otamita	75	B5
Otane	47	C3
Otangaroa	37	D3
Otangiwai	45	B4
Otanomomo	81	B4
Otao	39	A3
Otapiri	75	A5
Otara	47	D2
Otaraia	79	D2
Otaramarae	47	A2
Otatara	79	B2
Otaua	37	D4
Otautau	77	D5
Otehirinaki	49	A1
Otekaieke	71	B4
Otekura	81	B5
Otematata	71	A4
Oteramika	79	C2
Otewa	45	B2
Otiake	71	B4
Otikerama	75	C5
Otira	63	D4
Otokia	81	C3
Otoko	49	A3
Otonga	39	B4
Otoroa	37	D3
Otorohanga	45	B2
Otunui	45	B4
Oturoa	47	A2
Oturu	37	C3
Otuwhare	49	A1
Otway	43	B5
Oue	37	C4
Oueroa	53	A3
Ouruhia	69	C2
Outram	81	C3
Overdale	69	A3
Owahanga	55	D2
Owairaka Valley	45	C2
Owaka Valley	81	A5
Owaka	81	B5
Oware	79	D2
Owen Junction	59	B4
Owen River	59	B4
Owhango	45	B4
Owhata	37	B3
Owhiro	45	A2
Oxford	69	B1
Paekakariki	57	B3
Paemako	45	A3
Paenga	59	B5
Paerata	41	D4
Paerau	81	B2
Paeroa	43	B5
Paewhenua	45	C2
Pahi	41	B1
Pahia	79	A2
Pahiatua	55	B2
Pahou	47	C2
Paiaka	39	A4
Paihia	39	A3
Pakaraka	39	A3
Pakawau	59	C1
Pakeho	45	B2
Pakihikura	52	B3
Pakipaki	53	A2
Pakiri	41	D1
Pakotai	37	D4
Pakowhai	53	B2
Pakuratahi Forks	55	A4
Pakuratahi	55	A4
Palm Beach	41	D3
Palmerston North	55	B1
Palmerston	81	D2
Pamapuria	37	C3
Panetapu	45	C2
Pangatotara	59	C3
Panguru	37	C3
Papaaroha	43	B3
Papakai	45	C5
Papakaio	71	C5
Papakura	41	D4
Papamoa Beach	47	A1
Papamoa	47	A1
Papanui Junction	52	B2
Papanui	69	C2
Paparangi	51	D4
Paparata	41	D4
Paparimu	43	A4
Paparore	37	C2
Papatawa	55	C1
Papatea	49	A1
Papatoetoe	41	D3
Papatotara	77	C5
Papatowai	81	A5
Papawai	55	A4
Paponga	37	C3
Papua	37	C4
Papueru	47	C4
Papuni	47	D4
Para	61	B3
Paradise	75	A1
Parakai	41	C2
Parakao	39	A4
Parakiwai	43	C4
Parapara	37	C2
Paraparaumu	57	C3
Parawa	75	B4
Parawera	45	C2
Parekarangi	47	A3
Parekura Bay	39	B3
Paremata	49	B3
Pareora West	71	C3
Pareora	71	D3
Paretai	81	B4
Parewanui	55	A1
Parikawa	67	D2
Parikino	51	D4
Pariokara	49	A1
Park Hill	75	C4
Parnassus	67	B4
Paroa Bay	39	A3
Paroa	47	C2
Parua Bay	39	B5
Patangata	53	A3
Pataua North	39	B4
Patea	51	C4
Patearoa	81	C1
Paterangi	45	B1

Patetonga	43	B5
Patoka	52	D1
Patons Rock	59	C2
Patuki	61	B2
Patumahoe	41	D4
Paturau River	59	B1
Patutahi	49	A4
Paua	37	B1
Pauanui	43	C4
Pauatahanui	57	B4
Pawarenga	37	C3
Peebles	71	C5
Peel Forest	68	B3
Peep-O-Day	52	B3
Peggioh	61	B5
Pehiri	47	D4
Peketa	67	C3
Pelorus Bridge	61	A3
Pemberton	52	B3
Pendarves	68	C3
Pentland Hills	71	C4
Pepepe	41	D5
Peria	37	C3
Petone	57	B4
Phoebe	67	B4
Piarere	45	C1
Picton	61	B3
Pigeon Bay	69	C3
Pigeon Bush	55	A4
Piha	41	C3
Pihama	51	A4
Pikiwahine	39	A5
Pikopiko	77	D5
Pine Bush	79	D2
Pinedale	45	D2
Piopio	45	B3
Pios Beach	43	C5
Pipiriki	51	D4
Pipiroa	43	B4
Pipiwai	39	A4
Piriaka	45	B4
Pirinoa	55	A4
Piripai	47	C2
Piripaua	47	C4
Piripiri	45	A2
Pirongia	45	B1
Piropiro	45	B3
Pleasant Point	71	C3
Pleasant Valley	68	A4
Pleckville	55	B2
Plimmerton	57	B4
Poerua	63	D3
Pohangina	55	B1
Pohara Marae	45	C2
Pohara	59	C2
Pohatukura	49	B2
Pohokura	51	C3
Pohonui	52	B2
Pohuehue	41	C2
Pokaka	45	B5
Pokapu	39	A4
Pokeno	41	D4
Pokororo	59	C3
Pokuru	45	B2
Pollok	41	D4
Pomahaka	75	C5
Pomarangai	45	A2
Ponatahi	55	B4
Pongakawa Valley	47	B2
Pongakawa	47	B1
Pongaroa	55	C2
Ponsonby	41	C3
Poolburn	81	B1
Popotunoa	75	D5
Poraiti	53	A2
Porangahau	53	A4
Porewa	52	A3
Pori	55	C2
Porirua East	57	B4
Porirua	57	B4
Porootarao	45	B3
Poroti	39	A5
Poroutawhao	55	A2
Port Albert	41	C1
Port Chalmers	81	D3
Port Charles	43	B2
Port Fitzroy	43	B1
Port Jackson	43	A2
Port Levy	69	C2
Port Molyneux	81	B4
Port Motueka	59	D3
Port Ohope	47	C2
Port Puponga	59	C1
Port Robinson	67	B4
Port Waikato	41	C5
Portland	39	B5
Portobello	81	D3
Potaka	49	B1
Pouawa	49	B4
Poukawa	53	A2
Pounawea	81	B5
Pourerere	53	A3
Pouto	41	B1
Progress Junction	65	B2
Puaha	69	C3
Puha	49	A3
Puhata	37	C3
Puhoi	41	C2
Pukahu	53	A2
Pukearuhe	51	C2
Pukeatua	45	C2
Pukeawa	75	D5
Pukehiki	81	D3
Pukehina	47	B1
Pukehou	52	D3
Pukehuia	39	A5
Pukekapia	41	D5
Pukekawa	41	D4
Pukekohe	41	D4
Pukekura	45	C1
Pukemiro	37	C3
Pukemoremore	45	C1
Pukemutu	75	A5
Pukengahu	51	B3
Pukenui	37	B2
Pukeokahu	52	C2
Pukeoware	41	D4
Pukepito	75	D5
Pukepoto	37	C3
Pukerangi	81	C2
Pukerau	75	C5
Pukerimu	45	B1
Pukerua Bay	57	B3
Puketapu	53	A2
Puketeraki	81	D2
Puketi	37	D3
Puketitiri	52	D1
Puketoi	55	C2
Puketona	39	A3
Puketotara	45	B2
Puketui	43	B4
Puketurua	45	C2
Puketutu	45	B3
Pukeuri	71	C5
Punakaiki	63	D1
Punakitere	37	D4
Punaruku	39	B3
Punawai	68	B3
Pungaere	37	D3
Pungarehu	51	A3
Pungataua	52	B2
Puni	41	D4
Puniho	51	A3
Puniwhakau	51	C3
Puponga	59	C1
Pupuke	37	D3
Purakauiti	81	B5
Purakaunui	81	B5
Puramahoi	59	C2
Purangi	51	C3
Purekireki	81	A4
Pureora	45	C3
Purerua	39	A3
Puriri	43	B4
Purua	39	A4
Pururu	45	B2
Putara	55	B2
Putaruru	45	D2
Putorino	47	C5
Pyes Pa	47	A1
Pyramid Valley	65	D5
Pyramid	75	B5
Quarry Hills	79	D3
Queens Flat	71	B5
Queensberry	73	B5
Queenstown	75	B2
Racecourse Hill	69	A2
Raes Junction	75	D4
Raetihi	52	A1
Raglan	45	A1
Rahanui	45	A1
Rahotu	51	A3
Rai Valley	61	A3
Raio	37	B2
Rakahouka	79	C2
Rakaia Huts	69	B3
Rakaia	69	A3
Rakau	59	C4
Rakaunui	55	C2
Rakauroa	47	D3
Rakautara	67	C2
Rakautatahi	52	C3
Ramanui	45	A5
Ramarama	41	D4
Ranana	51	D4
Ranfurly	81	C1
Rangataua	52	A1
Rangiahua	37	D3
Rangiaowhia	45	B1
Rangiatea	45	B2
Rangihaeata	59	C2
Rangikura	51	C4
Rangiora	37	C3
Rangipo	45	C5
Rangipu	45	A1
Rangiputa	37	C2
Rangiriri	43	A5
Rangitaiki	47	A4
Rangitata Island	68	B4
Rangitata	68	B4
Rangitatau	51	C4
Rangitihi	37	C3
Rangitoto	45	B2
Rangitukia	49	C1
Rangitumau	55	B3
Rangiwaea Junction	52	B2
Rangiwahia	52	B3
Rankleburn	75	D5
Ranui	45	A1
Raoriaka	51	D4
Rapahoe	63	C2
Rapanui	51	D5
Rapaura	61	B4
Rapuwai	68	A4
Rarangi	61	B4
Raroa	47	C2
Rata	52	A3
Ratana	51	D5
Ratanui	81	B5
Ratapiko	51	B3
Raukawa	52	D2
Raukokore	49	B1
Raumai	55	B1
Raumati Beach	57	C3
Raumati South	57	C3
Raumati	55	C1
Raupo	41	B1
Raupunga	47	C5
Raurimu	45	B5
Rawene	37	C4
Rawhia	37	D3
Rawhiti	39	B3
Rawhitiroa	51	B3
Raymonds Gap	77	D5
Red Beach	41	C2
Redan	79	D2
Redvale	41	C2
Redwood Valley	59	D3
Redwood	57	B4
Reefton	65	B2
Reena	37	C4
Rehutai	37	D5
Reidston	81	D1
Remuera Settlement	37	D3
Renown	41	D5
Renwick	61	B4
Reotahi Bay	39	B5
Reporoa	47	A3
Reporua	49	C2
Rere	47	D4
Rerewhakaaitu	47	B3
Retaruke Upper	45	B5
Retaruke	45	B5
Rewa	52	B3
Rewarewa	45	B2
Richmond Downs	45	C1
Richmond	59	D3
Rimu	79	C2
Ringway	77	D5
Riponui	39	A4
Ripponvale	75	C2
Rissington	53	A1
Riverhead	41	C3
Riverlands	61	B4
Riversdale Beach	55	C4
Riversdale	75	B5
Riverton	79	B2
Riwaka	59	C3
Roa	63	D2
Rock and Pillar	81	C1
Rockford	69	A1
Rockville	59	C2
Rokeby	68	C3
Rolleston	69	B2
Romahapa	81	B4
Rongahere	75	D5
Rongoiti Junction	52	B2
Rongokokako	55	B2
Rongomai	55	B2
Roslyn Bush	79	C2
Ross	63	B4
Rotherham	67	A4
Rotoiti	47	B2
Rotokakahi	37	C3
Rotokawa	47	A2
Rotokino	63	A5
Rotokohu	59	A5
Rotomahana	47	A3
Rotomanu	63	D3
Rotongata	45	C2
Rotoorangi	45	C1
Rotoroa	59	B5
Rotorua	47	A2
Rototuna	41	B1
Rotowaro	41	D5
Round Hill	81	B3
Rowan	51	B3
Roxburgh Hydro	75	C3
Roxburgh	75	C3
Ruahine	52	B3
Ruakaka	39	B5
Ruakituri	47	D4
Ruakokoputuna	55	A4
Ruamahanga	43	B3
Ruanui	52	B2
Ruapekapeka	39	A4
Ruapuke	45	A1
Ruapuna	68	B3
Ruarangi	39	B5
Ruaroa	55	C1
Ruatahuna	47	C4
Ruataniwha	52	D3
Ruatapu	63	C4
Ruatiti	45	B5
Ruatoki North	47	C2
Ruatoria	49	C2
Ruawai	41	B1
Ruawaro	41	D5
Ruawhata	55	B2
Rukuhia	45	B1
Runanga	63	C2
Runaruna	37	C3
Runciman	41	D4
Russell	39	A3
Russells Flat	68	C2
Rutherglen	63	C3
Ryal Bush	79	C2
Salisbury	71	C3
Saltwater Creek	69	C1
Sandy Knolls	69	B2
Sandys Bay	39	B4
Sanson	55	A1
Santoft	55	A1
Scarborough	71	D3
Scargill	67	A4
Scotts Gap	77	D5
Scroggs Hill	81	C3
Seacliff	81	D2
Seadown	71	D3
Seafield	68	C3
Seaford	59	C1
Seaforth	71	D3
Seagrove	41	D4
Seatoun	57	B4
Seaward Downs	79	D2
Seddon	61	B4
Seddonville	59	A4
Sedgemere	69	B3
Sefton	69	C1
Selwyn Huts	69	B3
Selwyn	45	D1
Sergeants Hill	65	B1
Shaftesbury	43	B5
Shag Point	81	D2
Shag Valley	81	D1
Shannon	55	A2
Sheffield	69	A2
Shelly Beach	41	C2
Shenandoah	59	B5
Sherenden	52	D2
Sherwood Downs	71	C2
Shingle Creek	75	C3
Shirley	69	C2
Silverdale	41	C2
Six Mile	59	B5
Slope Point	79	D2
Smithfield	71	D3
Snells Beach	41	C2
South Bay	67	C3
South Beach	63	C3
South Head	41	B2
South Malvern	68	C2
Southbridge	69	B3
Southshore	69	C2
Spar Bush	79	B2
Spencerville	69	C2
Spotswood	67	B4
Spreydon	69	C2
Spring Creek	61	B4
Spring Grove	59	D4
Springbank	69	B1
Springbrook	71	C3
Springburn	68	B3
Springdale	43	B5
Springfield	39	B5
Springhill	52	D3
Springhills	79	C2
Springs Junction	65	C3
Springston	69	B2
St Andrews	71	C4
St Arnaud	59	C5
St Bathans	73	C5
St Patricks	75	B4
Stafford	63	C3
Stanley Brook	59	C3
Stanway	52	A3
Staveley	68	B3
Stewarts Gully	69	C2
Stillwater	41	C2
Stirling	81	B4
Stockton	59	A4
Stoke	59	D3
Stoneburn	81	D2
Stony Creek	81	B4
Strachans	71	B4
Stratford	51	B3
Strathmore	51	C3
Struan	71	B4
Summer Hill	81	B4
Summerhill	69	B1
Summerlea	59	A4
Sutherlands	71	C3
Sutton	81	C2
Swanson	41	C3
Swyncombe	67	C3
Tablelands	55	B4
Tadmor	59	C4
Tahaia	45	B2
Tahakopa	81	A5
Taharoa	45	A2
Tahatika	81	A5
Taheke	37	D4
Tahekeroa	41	C2
Tahere	39	B4
Tahora	45	A4
Tahoraiti	55	C1
Tahorakuri	47	A3
Tahuna	43	B5
Tahunga	47	D4
Taieri Beach	81	C4
Taieri Mouth	81	C3
Taihape	52	B2
Taiharuru	39	B5
Taihoa	45	D1
Taikirau	39	A4
Taikorea	55	A1
Taimate	61	C5
Taingaehe	41	B1
Taipa	37	C2
Taipuha	39	B5
Tairua	43	C3
Taitapu	69	C3
Takahue	37	C3
Takaka	59	C2
Takamatua	69	D3
Takamore	49	C2
Takapau	49	B2
Takapuna	41	D3
Takaputahi	49	A2
Takou Bay	39	A3
Takutai	63	C3
Tanatana	47	C2
Tane	55	B2
Taneatua	47	C2
Tanehopuwai	45	B3
Tanekaha	39	B4
Tangarakau	45	A4
Tangihua	39	A5
Tangimoana	55	A1
Tangiteroria	39	A5
Tangitu	45	B3
Tangiwai	52	B1
Tangoake	37	B1
Tangoio	53	B1
Tangowahine	39	A5
Taniwha	43	A5
Tanoa	41	B1
Tanupara	52	A1
Taoroa Junction	52	C2
Taotaoroa	45	C1
Tapanui	75	C5
Tapapa	45	D1
Tapawera	59	C3
Tapora	41	B1
Tapu	43	B3
Tapuhi	39	B4
Tapui	71	B5
Tapuwae	37	C3
Tara	41	C1
Taradale	53	A2
Tarakohe	59	C2
Taramakau	63	C3
Tarapatiki	47	C4
Tarara	81	B5
Tararu	43	B4
Tarata	51	B3
Tarawera	47	B5
Tariki	51	B3
Taringamotu	45	B4
Taronui Bay	39	A3
Tarras	73	B5
Tarurutangi	51	B2
Tasman	59	D3
Tataiahapi Pa	47	C2
Tataraimaka	51	A3
Tataramoa	55	C1
Tatare	63	A5
Tatuanui	43	B5
Tauhei	43	B5
Tauhoa	41	C2
Taumarunui	45	B4
Taumutu	69	B3
Taupaki	41	C3
Taupiri	43	A5
Taupo Bay	37	D2
Taupo	45	D4
Tauranga Bay	37	D2
Tauranga	47	A1
Tauranganui	41	D4
Taurangaruru	41	D4
Tauraroa	39	B5
Taurewa	45	C5
Tautoro	37	D4
Tauweru	55	B3
Tauwhare	45	C1
Tauwhareparae	49	B3
Tawa	61	D3
Tawai	71	C5
Tawanui	81	A5
Tawataia	55	B2
Tawhana	47	C3
Tawharanui	41	D2
Tawharemanuka	47	C3
Tawhata	45	B5
Taylorville	63	D2
Te Ahuahu	37	D3
Te Akatarawa	71	A4
Te Akatea	41	D5
Te Anau Downs	77	D2
Te Anau	77	D3
Te Anga	45	A2
Te Aputa	45	D4
Te Arai Point	41	C1
Te Arai	41	C1
Te Araroa	49	C1
Te Ariuru	49	C2
Te Aroha	43	B5
Te Awa	68	B4
Te Awamutu	45	B1
Te Awanga	53	B2
Te Hapua	37	B1
Te Haroto	47	B5
Te Hauke	53	A2
Te Henga	41	C3
Te Hihi	41	D4
Te Hoe	43	A5
Te Horo Beach	57	C3
Te Horo	57	C3
Te Houka	81	B4
Te Huahua	37	C3
Te Hutewai	45	A1
Te Iringa	37	D4
Te Kaha	49	A1
Te Kao	37	B1
Te Karae	37	C3
Te Karaka	49	A3
Te Kauwhata	43	A5
Te Kawa West	45	B2
Te Kawa	45	B2
Te Kinga	63	D3
Te Kiri	51	A3
Te Kohanga	41	D4
Te Kopua	45	B2
Te Koraha	45	A2
Te Kouma	43	B3
Te Koura	45	B4
Te Kowhai	41	B1
Te Kuha	65	B1
Te Kuiti	45	B2
Te Kumi	45	B2

Name	Page	Grid
Te Mahia	61	B3
Te Mahoe	47	B2
Te Maika	45	A2
Te Maire	45	B4
Te Mapara	45	B3
Te Mata	43	B3
Te Matai	47	A1
Te Miro	45	C1
Te Moana	68	A4
Te Namu	59	A3
Te Ngae	47	A2
Te Pahu	45	B1
Te Paki	37	A1
Te Papatapu	45	A1
Te Peka	79	D2
Te Pene	39	A3
Te Pirita	68	C2
Te Pohue	53	A1
Te Poi	45	D1
Te Popo	51	B3
Te Pouwhakatutu	45	D3
Te Pu	47	A2
Te Pua	41	C2
Te Puia Springs	49	C2
Te Puke	47	A1
Te Puninga	43	B5
Te Puru	43	B4
Te Rahu	45	B1
Te Raina	45	D4
Te Ranga	45	D1
Te Rapa	61	B5
Te Rapa	67	D1
Te Rauamoa	45	B2
Te Raumauku	45	B2
Te Reinga	47	D4
Te Rerenga	43	B3
Te Rore	37	C3
Te Roti	51	B4
Te Rou	61	A4
Te Taho	63	B5
Te Teko	47	B2
Te Tii	39	A3
Te Tipua	79	D1
Te Toro	41	D4
Te Tua	77	D5
Te Tuhi Junction	51	D4
Te Tumu	47	A1
Te Uku	45	A1
Te Uri	55	D1
Te Waewae	77	D5
Te Waiiti	47	C4
Te Wairoa	47	A2
Te Waitere	45	A2
Te Wera	51	C3
Te Whaiti	47	B4
Te Whanga	55	B3
Te Wharau	37	D5
Te Whau	37	D3
Te Whetu	45	D2
Teddington	69	C3
Tekapo Military Camp	71	A2
Temple View	45	B1
Templeton	69	B2
Temuka	71	D3
Tennyson Inlet	61	B3
Teschemakers	81	D1
Teviot	81	A2
Thames	43	B4
The Five Bridges	49	B3
The Forks	63	A5
The Kaik	69	D3
The Key	77	D3
The Pines Beach	69	C2
The Plateau	55	A4
The Point	68	C2
The Rocks	79	B2
Thomsons Crossing	79	C2
Thornbury	79	B2
Thornton	47	C2
Thorpe	59	C3
Three Mile Bush	39	B4
Ti Point	41	D1
Ti Tree Point	55	D2
Tihiroa	45	B2
Tihoi	45	C3
Tikinui	41	B1
Tikitiki	49	C1
Tikokino	52	D3
Tikorangi	51	B2
Timaru	71	D3
Timpanys	79	C2
Tiniroto	47	D4
Tinui	55	C3
Tinwald	68	C3
Tirau	45	C1
Tiraumea	55	C2
Tiriraukawa	52	B2
Tirohanga	47	D2
Tirohia	43	B5
Tiroiti	81	C1
Tiromoana	63	D1
Tisbury	79	C2
Titahi Bay	57	B4
Titiroa	79	D2
Titoki	39	A5
Toatoa	47	D2
Tohunga Junction	52	A1
Toi Flat	55	D1
Toiro	81	B4
Tokaanu	45	D4
Tokanui	45	B2
Tokaora	51	B4
Tokarahi	71	C5
Tokata	49	C1
Tokatoka	41	B1
Tokerau Beach	37	C2
Toko Mouth	81	C4
Toko	51	B3
Tokoiti	81	B4
Tokomaru Bay	49	C2
Tokomaru	55	B2
Tokorangi	52	A3
Tokoroa	45	D2
Tolaga Bay	49	B3
Tomarata	41	C1
Tongaporutu	51	C2
Tongariro	45	D4
Tophouse	59	C5
Topuni	41	C1
Tora	55	B5
Torbay	41	D2
Torehape	43	B4
Torere	47	D2
Totara Flat	63	D2
Totara North	37	D2
Totara Valley	71	C3
Totaranui	59	D2
Towai	39	A4
Trentham	71	C2
Tryphena	43	B1
Tuahiwi	69	C1
Tuakau	41	D4
Tuamarina	61	B4
Tuamata	75	D5
Tuapeka Flat	75	D5
Tuapeka Mouth	75	D5
Tuapeka West	75	D5
Tuatapere	77	D5
Tuateawa	43	B2
Tuhara	47	D5
Tuhikaramea	45	B1
Tuhitarata	55	A4
Tuhua	45	B4
Tui	59	C4
Tukemokihi	47	D5
Tukino	45	C5
Tumahu	51	A3
Tumai	81	D2
Tumunui	47	A3
Tuparoa	49	C2
Turakina	51	D5
Turangarere	52	B2
Turangi	45	D4
Turitea	55	B2
Turiwhate	63	D3
Turiwiri	39	A5
Turua	43	B4
Tussock Creek	79	C2
Tutaematai	39	B3
Tutaenui	52	A3
Tutaki	59	B5
Tutamoe	37	D4
Tutira	53	B1
Tutukaka	39	B4
Tuturau	79	D2
Tuturumuri	55	A5
Tututawa	51	C3
Twin Bridges	37	D4
Twizel	71	A3
Umawera	37	D3
Umere	59	A3
Umutaoroa	55	C1
Umutoi	52	C3
Upokongaro	51	D5
Upper Atiamuri	45	D2
Upper Hutt	57	C4
Upper Kawhatau	55	B5
Upper Matakitaki	59	B5
Upper Moutere	59	D3
Upper Takaka	59	C2
Upper Waitati	81	D3
Upper Waitohi	68	A4
Urenui	51	B2
Uretane	71	C4
Uruti	51	C2
Uruwhenua	59	C2
Utiku	52	B2
Utuwai	52	B3
Valetta	68	B3
View Hill	69	A1
Vinegar Hill	52	B3
Waddington	69	A2
Waerenga	43	A4
Waerengaokuri	49	A4
Waharoa	45	C1
Waianakarua	81	D1
Waiare	37	D3
Waiariari	71	C4
Waiarikiki	79	D2
Waiaro	43	B2
Waiaruhe	55	C1
Waiatarua	41	C3
Waiatoto	76	D1
Waiau Pa	41	D4
Waiau	67	B4
Waiaua	47	D2
Waihaha	39	B3
Waihao Downs	71	C4
Waihaorunga	71	B4
Waiharakeke	43	C4
Waihau Bay	49	B1
Waihi Beach	43	C5
Waihi Gorge	68	A4
Waihi	43	C5
Waihirere	49	B4
Waihoaka	79	D2
Waihoki Valley	55	C2
Waihola	81	C3
Waihopo	37	B1
Waihou Valley	37	D3
Waihou	43	B5
Waihua	47	C5
Waihue	37	D5
Waihuka	37	D3
Wai-iti	59	D4
Waikaia	75	B4
Waikaka Valley	75	C5
Waikaka	75	C5
Waikakahi	71	C4
Waikana	79	D2
Waikanae Beach	57	C3
Waikanae	57	C3
Waikaraka	39	B5
Waikare	39	B3
Waikaremoana	47	C4
Waikaretu	41	D5
Waikari	65	D5
Waikato	59	C1
Waikawa Beach	55	A2
Waikawa	61	B3
Waikawau	43	B2
Waikeria	45	B2
Waikiekie	39	B5
Waikino	43	B5
Waikirikiri	47	C2
Waikite Valley	47	A3
Waikite	47	A3
Waikoau	53	A1
Waikoikoi	75	C5
Waikorea	41	D5
Waikouaiti	81	D2
Waikoukou Valley	41	C3
Waikouro	77	D5
Waikuku Beach	69	C1
Waikuku	69	C1
Waikune	45	B5
Waima	37	D4
Waimahaka	79	D2
Waimahana	47	A3
Waimahora	45	B2
Waimamaku	37	C4
Waimana	47	C2
Waimangaroa	65	B1
Waimangu	47	A3
Waimanoni	37	C2
Waimarama	53	B3
Waimata	43	C5
Waimate	71	C4
Waimatenui	37	D4
Waimatua	79	C2
Waimatuku	79	B2
Waimauku	41	C3
Waimaunga	65	B2
Waimiha	45	B3
Waimihia	47	A4
Waimiro	55	C2
Waimotu	81	D1
Waimumu	75	B5
Waingake	49	A4
Waingarara	47	C2
Waingawa	55	B3
Wainihinihi	63	D3
Wainui Junction	37	B3
Wainui	37	D2
Wainuiomata	57	B4
Wainuioru	55	B3
Waioeka Pa	47	D2
Waiohau	47	B2
Waiohiki	53	A2
Waiomatatini	49	C1
Waiomio	39	A4
Waiomu	43	B3
Waione	55	D2
Waioneke	41	B2
Waiorore	49	A1
Waiotahi Beach	47	D2
Waiotahi Valley	47	C2
Waiotahi	47	D2
Waiotama	39	A5
Waiotapu	47	A3
Waiotehue	37	C3
Waiotemarama	37	C4
Waiotira	39	A5
Waiotu	39	B4
Waiouru	52	B1
Waipa Valley	45	B3
Waipa Village	47	A2
Waipahi	75	C5
Waipaipai	39	B4
Waipango	79	B2
Waipaoa	49	A3
Waipapa	37	D3
Waipapakauri Beach	37	B2
Waipara	67	A5
Waiparera	39	B5
Waiparu	75	B4
Waipatiki Beach	53	B1
Waipatiki	55	D2
Waipawa	52	D3
Waipiata	81	C1
Waipipi	41	D4
Waipiro Bay	49	C2
Waipopo	71	D3
Waipori Falls	81	B3
Waipoua Forest	37	C4
Waipoua Settlement	37	C4
Waipounamu	75	B4
Waipu Caves	39	B5
Waipu	39	B5
Waipukurau	52	D3
Waipuna	65	B3
Waipuru	52	B3
Wairakau	43	B5
Wairakei Village	45	D3
Wairakei	45	D3
Wairamarama	41	D5
Wairapukao	47	B3
Wairau Bar	61	B4
Wairau Pa	61	B4
Wairau Valley	61	A4
Waireia	37	C4
Waireka	47	A3
Wairio	77	D5
Wairoa	47	D5
Wairuna	75	C5
Wairunga	81	D2
Waitaanga	45	A4
Waitaha	63	B4
Waitahanui	45	D4
Waitahora	55	C1
Waitahu	65	B2
Waitahuna West	75	D5
Waitahuna	81	B3
Waitakaruru	43	A4
Waitakere	41	C3
Waitaki Bridge	71	C5
Waitane	79	C2
Waitangi	71	A4
Waitanguru	45	A3
Waitao	47	A1
Waitapu	59	C2
Waitara	51	B2
Waitarere	55	A2
Waitaria Bay	61	B3
Waitaruke	37	D3
Waitati	81	D3
Waitawa	71	C3
Waitawheta	43	B5
Waiteitei	41	C1
Waitekauri	43	B5
Waitepeka	81	B4
Waiterimu	43	A5
Waiteti	47	A2
Waitetoki	37	C2
Waitetoko	45	D4
Waitetuna	45	B1
Waiti	43	B5
Waitiki Landing	37	B1
Waitoa	43	B5
Waitohi	55	A1
Waitoki	41	C2
Waitomo Caves	45	B2
Waitomo Valley	45	B2
Waitotara	51	C4
Waituhi	49	A4
Waituna West	52	B3
Waituna	71	C4
Waiuku	41	D4
Waiuta	65	B3
Waiwaka	55	B2
Waiwera South	81	A4
Waiwera	41	C2
Waiwhare	52	D1
Waiwhiu	41	C1
Wakanui	68	C4
Wakapatu	79	A2
Wakapuaka	59	D3
Wakarara	52	C2
Wakefield	59	D4
Wallacetown	79	B2
Wallingford	53	A4
Wanaka	73	A5
Wangaloa	81	B4
Wanganui	51	D5
Wanstead	55	D1
Waotu	45	C2
Ward	61	C5
Warea	51	A3
Warepa	81	B4
Warkworth	41	C2
Waro	39	B4
Warrington	81	D2
Washdyke	71	C3
Waterton	68	C4
Waverley	51	C4
Wawa	45	D2
Wayby Valley	41	C1
Weber	55	D2
Wedderburn	71	A5
Weedons	69	B2
Wekaweka	37	C4
Welcome Bay	47	A1
Welds Hill	61	B5
Wellington	57	B4
Wellsford	41	C1
Wendon	75	B4
West Eyreton	69	B2
West Melton	69	B2
West Plains	79	B2
Westerfield	68	B3
Westmere	43	A5
Weston	71	C5
Westport	65	B1
Westshore	53	B2
Weymouth	41	D4
Whakaihuwhaka	51	D2
Whakaki	47	D5
Whakamaru	45	C3
Whakapapa Village	45	C5
Whakapara	39	B4
Whakapirau	41	B1
Whakapourangi	49	B2
Whakarae	47	C3
Whakarau	49	A3
Whakaronga	55	B1
Whakataki	55	C3
Whakatane	47	B2
Whakatete Bay	43	B4
Whakatiwai	43	A4
Whakatu	53	B2
Whakawhitira	49	C1
Whananaki	39	B4
Whanarua Bay	49	A1
Whanawhana	52	D2
Whangae	39	A3
Whangaehu	51	D5
Whangaimoana	55	A5
Whangamarino	43	A4
Whangamata	43	C4
Whangamomona	45	C4
Whanganui	45	D4
Whangaparaoa	41	D2
Whangaparapara	43	B1
Whangape	37	C3
Whangaporoto	45	D4
Whangapoua	43	B3
Whangara	49	B4
Whangarata	41	D4
Whangarei	39	B5
Whangaripo	41	C1
Whangaruru North	39	B3
Whangaruru	39	B3
Whangateau	41	D1
Wharanui	61	B5
Whare Flat	81	C3
Whareama	55	C3
Wharehine	41	C1
Wharehuanui	75	B2
Wharehuia	51	B3
Wharekaka	49	B3
Wharekauhau	57	C4
Wharekawa	43	C4
Wharekohe	39	A5
Wharekopae	47	D4
Whareora	39	B4
Wharepaina	47	A3
Wharepapa	41	C3
Wharepapo	43	B4
Wharepo	49	C2
Wharepuhunga	45	C2
Wharetoa	75	D5
Whareweka	45	D4
Wharua	71	B4
Whataroa	63	A5
Whatatutu	49	A3
Whatawhata	45	B1
Whatipu	41	C3
Whatitiri	39	A5
Whatuwhiwhi	37	C2
Wheatstone	68	C4
Whenuahou	52	C3
Whenuakite	43	C3
Whenuapai	41	C3
Whetukura	55	D1
Whirinaki	37	C4
Whiritoa	43	C4
Whiriwhiri	41	D4
White Rock	65	D5
Whitecliffs	68	C2
Whitehall	45	C1
Whitemans Valley	57	C4
Whiterigg	75	C5
Whitford	41	D3
Whitianga	43	B3
Whitikahu	43	A5
Whitikau	47	D2
Willow Flat	47	C5
Willowbank	75	C5
Willowbridge	71	C4
Willowby	68	C4
Willowford	52	D1
Wilsons Crossing	79	C2
Wiltsdown	45	D2
Wimbledon	55	D2
Winchester	68	B4
Winchmore	68	C3
Windsor	71	B5
Windwhistle	68	C2
Windy Hill	39	A5
Winiata	52	B2
Winscombe	71	B2
Winslow	68	C3
Winton	75	A5
Woodbourne	61	B4
Woodbury	68	A4
Woodcocks	41	C2
Woodend Beach	69	C1
Woodend	69	C1
Woodhill	41	C3
Woodlands	43	C5
Woodlaw	77	D5
Woodleigh	41	D5
Woodside	81	C3
Woodstock	59	C3
Woodville	55	C1
Wreys Bush	75	A5
Wrights Bush	79	B2
Wyllies Crossing	81	C3
Wyndham	79	D2